D0727894

BIRDS *of* DETROIT

Chris C. Fisher
Allen T. Chartier

LONE
PINE

© 1997 by Lone Pine Publishing
First printed in 1997   10 9 8 7 6 5 4 3 2 1
Printed in Canada

All rights reserved. No part of this work covered by the copyrights hereon may
be reproduced or used in any form or by any means—graphic, electronic or
mechanical—without the prior written permission of the publisher, except
for reviewers, who may quote brief passages. Any request for photocopying,
recording, taping or storage on information retrieval systems of any part of this
work shall be directed in writing to the publisher.

The Publisher: Lone Pine Publishing

1901 Raymond Ave. SW, Suite C	206, 10426 – 81 Ave.	202A, 1110 Seymour St.
Renton, WA 98055	Edmonton, AB T6E 1X5	Vancouver, BC V6B 3N3
USA	Canada	Canada

Canadian Cataloguing in Publication Data

Fisher, Chris C. (Christopher Charles), date–
    Birds of Detroit

    Includes bibliographical references and index.
    ISBN 1-55105-126-5

    1. Birds—Michigan—Detroit—Identification. 2. Bird
watching—Michigan—Detroit. I. Chartier, Allen, 1957–
II. Title.
QL684.M5F57 1997   598'.09774'34   C97-910643-5

Senior Editor: Nancy Foulds
Project Editor: Roland Lines
Research Assistant: Eloise Pulos
Technical Review: Wayne Campbell
Production Manager: David Dodge
Production and Layout: Michelle Bynoe
Book Design: Carol S. Dragich
Cover Design: Jun Lee
Cover Illustration: Gary Ross
Map: Volker Bodegom
Illustrations: Gary Ross, Ted Nordhagen, Ewa Pluciennik
Separations and Film: Elite Lithographers Co. Ltd., Edmonton, Alberta, Canada
Printing: Quality Colour Press Inc., Edmonton, Alberta, Canada

The publisher gratefully acknowledges the assistance of the Department of Canadian
Heritage and Alberta Community Development, and the financial support provided by the
Alberta Foundation for the Arts.

Contents

Acknowledgments

A book such as this is made possible by the inspired work of Detroit's naturalist community, whose contributions continue to advance the science of ornithology and to motivate a new generation of nature lovers.

Our thanks go to Gary Ross and Ted Nordhagen, whose illustrations have elevated the quality of this book; to Carole Patterson, for her continual support; to the birding societies of the Detroit area, which all make daily contributions to natural history; to the team at Lone Pine Publishing—Roland Lines, Nancy Foulds, Eloise Pulos, Greg Brown, Michelle Bynoe and Shane Kennedy—for their input and steering; to John Acorn and Jim Butler, for their stewardship and their remarkable passion; and, finally, to Wayne Campbell, a premier naturalist whose works have served as models of excellence, for his thorough and helpful review of the text.

Introduction

No matter where we live, birds are a natural part of our lives. We are so used to seeing them that we often take their presence for granted, but when we take the time to notice their colors, songs and behaviors, we experience their dynamic appeal.

This book presents a brief introduction into the lives of birds. It is intended to serve as both a bird identification guide and a bird appreciation guide. Getting to know the names of birds is the first step toward getting to know birds. Once we've made contact with a species, we can better appreciate its character and mannerisms during future encounters. Over a lifetime of meetings, many birds become acquaintances, some seen daily, others not for years.

The selection of species within this book represents a balance between the familiar and the noteworthy. Many of the 125 species described in this guide are the most common species found in the Detroit area (Wayne, Oakland and Macomb counties). Some are less common, but they are noteworthy because they are important ecologically or because their particular status grants them a high profile. It would be impossible for a beginners' book such as this to comprehensively describe all the birds found in the Detroit area. Furthermore, there is no one site where all the species within this book can be observed simultaneously, but most species can be viewed—at least seasonally—within a short drive from Detroit.

It is hoped that this guide will inspire novice birdwatchers into spending some time outdoors, gaining valuable experience with the local bird community. This book stresses the identification of birds, but it also attempts to bring them to life by discussing their various character traits. We often discuss a bird's character traits in human terms, because personifying a bird's character can help us to feel a bond with the birds. The perceived links with birds should not be mistaken for actual behaviors, however, because our interpretations may falsely reflect the complexities of bird life.

FEATURES OF THE LANDSCAPE

The variety of habitats around Detroit are home to a rich diversity of bird species. Although the Detroit area is relatively small in size, more than 300 of Michigan's 350 regularly occurring bird species have been found here. Situated along the Lake St. Clair and Detroit River system and within close proximity to the Great Lakes, the Detroit area is a favorite spot for a wide variety of bird life.

The lakeshores and river valleys around the Detroit area act as natural pathways, funneling birds along their north-south migration routes. Stretches of beach and rocky shores strewn with pockets of deciduous forest provide habitat and foraging opportunities for many birds. Along these shorelines, sandpipers, geese, gulls, terns and other migrating waterbirds stop to replenish their energy supplies, moving from one productive foraging site to another. During fall, tens of thousands of hawks make their way through the Great Lakes, crossing into Michigan at the southern end of the Detroit River. The most numerous species is the Broad-winged Hawk—and the best place to watch these annual migrations is Lake Erie Metropark.

The flat and open areas of Wayne and Macomb counties are inhabited by many species of birds. The hedgerows, edge habitats and uncultivated grassy fields of the countryside provide warmth and shelter for a variety of migrants; during the breeding season, many species nest here in the vegetation. The more sparsely vegetated, drained farmlands that are common outside the Detroit area also attract birds. During spring and summer, look for Eastern Bluebirds or Vesper Sparrows foraging for seeds and insects along open fields and roadsides. The more rural areas of Macomb and Oakland counties are great places to see prairie bird species. Many prairie birds can still be found in rural southern Michigan, but there is no doubt that the draining of wetlands, the clearing of woodlots and the use of herbicides and pesticides have all contributed to a loss of bird life, while, sadly, most if not all of southern Michigan's native grasslands have all but disappeared.

With the disappearance of southern Michigan's second growth forests, the state parks, game areas and other public lands around Detroit have come to play an essential role in preserving biodiversity. These floodplains and impressive beech-maple forests provide valuable islands of habitat for the various vireos, warblers, thrushes, flycatchers and sparrows that are regular visitors to our area. Fairlane Woods, found alongside the Rouge River at the University of Michigan–Dearborn, is an ideal place to find migrating songbirds in spring and fall.

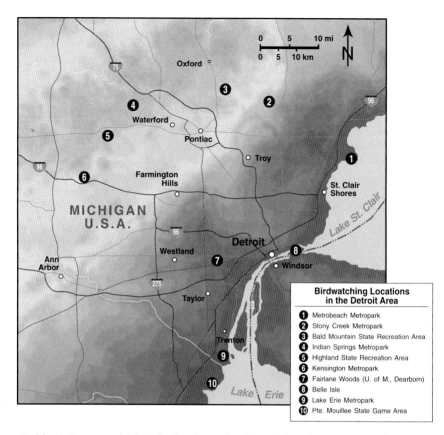

Birdwatching Locations in the Detroit Area

1. Metrobeach Metropark
2. Stony Creek Metropark
3. Bald Mountain State Recreation Area
4. Indian Springs Metropark
5. Highland State Recreation Area
6. Kensington Metropark
7. Fairlane Woods (U. of M., Dearborn)
8. Belle Isle
9. Lake Erie Metropark
10. Pte. Mouillee State Game Area

Oakland County, which is farther from the Great Lakes, has more varied terrain. It has numerous hills and vernal ponds, and the most extensive deciduous forests in the Detroit area. It is often much easier to see Ruffed Grouse, Scarlet Tanagers, Rose-breasted Grosbeaks and other birds in Oakland County than other parts of the Detroit area, which have only isolated pockets of trees. For an interesting array of both northern and southern breeding species, such as the Pileated Woodpecker, the American Redstart and the Hooded Warbler, visit Indian Springs Metropark and Highland State Recreation Area.

Detroit's city parks and backyards also attract bird life. Landscaped settings are often good places to become familiar with birds; many of the birds you will find in the Detroit area tend to overlook the noisy lifestyle of their human counterparts. Backyard feeders and nest boxes are a welcome invitation throughout winter, and during the warmer months, many birds take refuge in the city's broadleaf trees. Even within the city's most modified areas, you will find birds—those that are well adapted to urban areas, such as Rock Doves, House Sparrows and European Starlings.

THE IMPORTANCE OF HABITAT

Understanding the relationship between habitats and bird species often helps identify which birds are which. Because you won't find a loon up a tree or a quail out at sea, habitat is an important thing to note when birdwatching.

The quality of habitat is one of the most powerful factors to influence bird distribution, and with experience you may become amazed by the predictability of some birds within a specific habitat type. The habitat icons in this book represent the general environments where each species is most likely to be seen. It is important to realize, however, that because of their migratory habits, birds are sometimes found in completely different habitats. These unexpected surprises—despite being confusing to novice birders—are among the most powerful motivations for the increasing legion of birdwatchers.

Lakes and Open Water	Shorelines	Marshes and Wetlands
Fields and Shrubby Areas	Broadleaf Forests	Coniferous Forests
Parks and Gardens		

THE ORGANIZATION OF THIS BOOK

To simplify field identification, *Birds of Detroit* is organized slightly differently from many other field guides that use strict phylogenetic groupings. In cases where many birds from the same family are described, conventional groupings are maintained. In other cases, however, distantly related birds that share physical and behavioral similarities are grouped together. This blend of family groupings and groups of physically similar species strives to help the novice birdwatcher identify and appreciate the birds he or she encounters.

DIVING BIRDS

loons, grebes, cormorants

These heavy-bodied birds are adapted to diving for their food. Between their underwater foraging dives, they are most frequently seen on the surface of the water. These birds could only be confused with one another or with certain diving ducks.

WETLAND WADERS

herons, egrets, soras, coots

Although this group varies considerably in size and represents two separate families of birds, wetland waders share similar habitat and food preferences. Some of these long-legged birds of marshes are quite common, but certain species are heard far more than they are seen.

WATERFOWL

swans, geese, ducks

Waterfowl tend to have stout bodies, they have webbed feet, and they are swift in flight. Although most species are associated with water, waterfowl can sometimes be seen grazing on upland sites.

VULTURES, HAWKS AND FALCONS

vultures, hawks, kestrels

From deep forests to open country to large lakes, there are hawks and falcons hunting the skies. They have a predatory look—with sharp talons, a hooked bill and forward-facing eyes—which easily identifies members of this group. Hawks and vultures generally use their broad wings to soar in thermals and updrafts.

GROUSE AND QUAILS

These gamebirds superficially resemble chickens. They are stout birds and poor flyers, and they are most often encountered on the ground or when flushed.

SHOREBIRDS

killdeers, sandpipers, snipes, woodcocks

Although these small, long-legged, swift-flying birds are mainly found along shores, don't be surprised to find certain species in pastures and marshy areas.

GULLS AND TERNS

Gulls are relatively large, usually light-colored birds that are frequently seen swimming, walking about in urban areas or soaring gracefully over the city. Their backs tend to be darker than their bellies, and their feet are webbed. Terns are in the same family as gulls, but they are not often seen on the ground, they rarely soar and they have straight, pointed bills.

DOVES

Both of Detroit's doves are easily recognizable. Rock Doves are found in all urban areas, from city parks to the downtown core. These urban doves have many of the same physical and behavioral characteristics as the 'wilder' Mourning Doves.

NOCTURNAL BIRDS

owls, nighthawks

These night hunters all have large eyes. Owls, which primarily prey on rodents, have powerful, taloned feet and strongly hooked bills. Nighthawks, which catch moths and other nocturnal insects on the wing, have extremely large mouths. Although owls are primarily active at night, their distinctive calls enable bird watchers to readily identify them.

KINGFISHERS

The kingfisher's behavior and physical characteristics are quite unlike any other bird in Detroit. It primarily hunts fish, plunging after them from the air or from an overhanging perch.

WOODPECKERS

The drumming sound of hammering wood and their vertical foraging habits easily identify most woodpeckers. Even when these birds cannot be seen or heard, the characteristic marks of certain species can be seen on trees in any mature forest.

HUMMINGBIRDS

The Ruby-throated Hummingbird is Detroit's smallest bird. Its bright colors and swift flight are very characteristic.

FLYCATCHERS

wood-pewees, flycatchers, phoebes, kingbirds

These birds might be best identified by their foraging behavior. As their name implies, flycatchers catch insects on the wing, darting after them from a favorite perch. Many flycatchers have subdued plumage, but phoebes and kingbirds are rather boldly marked.

SWIFTS AND SWALLOWS

Members of these two families are typically seen at their nest sites or in flight. Small but sleek, swallows fly gracefully in pursuit of insects. Swifts are small, dark birds with long, narrow wings and short tails, and they have a more 'mechanical' flight behavior.

JAYS AND CROWS

Many members of this family are known for their intelligence and adaptability. They are easily observed birds that are frequently extremely bold, teasing the animal-human barrier. They are sometimes called 'corvids,' from Corvidae, the scientific name for the family.

SMALL SONGBIRDS

chickadees, nuthatches, wrens, kinglets

Birds in this group are all generally smaller than a sparrow. Many of them associate with one another in mixed-species flocks, and they are commonly encountered in city parks, backyards and other wooded areas.

BLUEBIRDS AND THRUSHES

bluebirds, thrushes, robins

From the bold robin to the secretive forest thrushes, this group of beautiful singers has the finest collective voice. Although some thrushes are very familiar, others require a little experience and patience to identify.

VIREOS AND WARBLERS

vireos, warblers, redstarts, yellowthroats

Warblers are splashed liberally with colors, whereas vireos tend to dress in pale olive. These birds are all very small and sing characteristic courtship songs.

MID-SIZED SONGBIRDS

tanagers, waxwings, starlings, etc.

The birds within this group are all sized between a sparrow and a robin. Tanagers are very colorful and sing complex, flute-like songs, but waxwings are more reserved in dress and voice. Starlings are frequently seen and heard all over our area.

SPARROWS

towhees, sparrows, juncos

These small, often indistinct birds are predominantly brown and streaky. Their songs are often very useful in identification. Many birdwatchers discount sparrows as 'little brown birds'—towhees are colorful exceptions—but they are worthy of the extra identification effort.

BLACKBIRDS AND ORIOLES

blackbirds, cowbirds, orioles, etc.

Most of these birds are predominantly black and have relatively long tails. They are common in open areas, city parks and agricultural fields. The Eastern Meadowlark belongs in the blackbird family, despite not being black and having a short tail.

FINCH-LIKE BIRDS

finches, cardinals, buntings, etc.

These finches and finch-like birds are primarily adapted to feeding on seeds, and they have stout, conical bills. Many are birdfeeder regulars, and they are a familiar part of the winter scene.

ABUNDANCE CHARTS

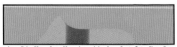

Accompanying each bird description is a chart that indicates the relative abundance of the species throughout the year. These stylized graphs offer some insight into the distribution and abundance of the birds, but they should not be viewed as definitive because they represent a generalized overview. There may be inconsistencies specific to time and location, but these charts should provide readers with a basic reference for bird abundance and occurrence.

Each chart is divided into the 12 months of the year. The pale orange that colors the chart is an indication of abundance: the higher the color, the more common the bird. Dark orange is used to indicate the nesting period. The time frame of breeding is approximate, however, and nesting birds can sometimes be found both before and after the period indicated on the chart. If no nesting color is shown, the bird breeds outside the Detroit area or visits Detroit during migration or during winter.

These graphs are based on personal observations and on local references.

abundant

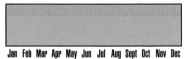
common

uncommon

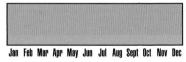
rare

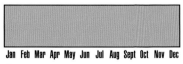
unlikely

absent

BIRDS
of
DETROIT

Common Loon
Gavia immer

The Common Loon is a noble symbol of northern wilderness, preferring the diminishing pristine areas where birds alone quarrel over naval rights-of-way. Loons do not breed in our area, but they visit each year during migration. Their intricate dark green and white breeding wardrobe gives way to winter browns. These birds can often be spotted offshore at Metro Beach Metropark in spring migration.

Loons routinely poke their heads underwater to look for potential prey and plot their forthcoming pursuit. They dive deeply and efficiently, compressing their feathers to reduce underwater drag and to decrease their buoyancy. Propelling themselves primarily with their legs, these birds manage to outswim fish over short distances. Because they have solid bones (unlike most other birds, which have hollow bones) and because their legs are placed well back on their bodies for diving, Common Loons require long stretches of open water for take-off. Some loons are fatally trapped by constricting ice as lakes freeze in late fall.

Similar Species: Common Merganser (p. 38) has an orange bill and very white plumage. Double-crested Cormorant (p. 20) has all-black plumage and a long neck, and it usually holds its bill pointed upward when it swims.

non-breeding

Quick I.D.: larger than a duck; sexes similar; stout, sharp bill. *In flight:* hunch-backed. *Breeding:* dark green hood; black-and-white checkerboard back; fine, white 'necklace.' *Non-breeding:* sandy-brown back; light underparts.
Size: 27–33 in.

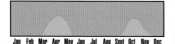

Jan Feb Mar Apr May Jun Jul Aug Sept Oct Nov Dec

Pied-billed Grebe
Podilymbus podiceps

The small, stout, drab body of the Pied-billed Grebe seems perfectly suited to its marshy habitat, but its loud, whooping *kuk-kuk-cow-cow-cow-cowp-cowp!* is a sound that seems more at home in a tropical rainforest. Pied-billed Grebes can be found on most freshwater wetlands that are surrounded by cattails, bulrushes or other emergent vegetation. These diving birds are frustrating to follow as they disappear and then re-appear among the water lilies at Metro Beach Metropark, Pointe Mouillee and other urban wetlands.

During summer, these small, reclusive grebes build nests that float on the water's surface, and their eggs often rest in waterlogged vegetation. Young grebes take their first swim soon after hatching, but they will instinctively clamber aboard a parent's back at the first sign of danger.

Similar Species: Horned Grebe has light underparts. Ducks have bills that are flattened top to bottom.

breeding

Quick I.D.: smaller than a duck; sexes similar; all brown. *Breeding:* dark vertical band on thick, white bill; black chin.
First year (summer/fall): striped brown and white.
Size: 12–14 in.

Jan Feb Mar Apr May Jun Jul Aug Sept Oct Nov Dec

Double-crested Cormorant
Phalacrocorax auritus

When Double-crested Cormorants are seen flying in single-file, low over Lake St. Clair or the Detroit River, the prehistoric sight hints to their ancestry. The tight, dark flocks soar and sail over lakes until hunger or the need for rest draws them to the water's surface. It is there that cormorants are most comfortable, disappearing beneath the surface in deep foraging dives.

Cormorants lack the ability to waterproof their feathers, so they need to dry their wings after each swim. They frequently perch on bridge pilings and buoys with their wings partially spread to expose their wet feathers to the sun and the wind. It would seem to be a great disadvantage for a waterbird to have to dry its wings, but the cormorant's ability to wet its feathers decreases the bird's buoyancy, making it easier for the cormorant to swim after the fish on which it preys. Sealed nostrils, a long, rudder-like tail and excellent underwater vision are other features of the cormorant's aquatic lifestyle.

Similar Species: Common Loon (p. 18) has a shorter neck and is more stout overall.

breeding

Quick I.D.: goose-sized; sexes similar; all black; long tail; long neck. *In flight:* kinked neck; rapid wing beats. *Breeding:* bright orange throat pouch; black plumes streaming back from eyebrows (seen only at close range). *First year:* brown; pale neck, breast and belly.
Size: 30–35 in.

Jan Feb Mar Apr May Jun Jul Aug Sept Oct Nov Dec

Great Blue Heron
Ardea herodias

breeding

The Great Blue Heron is one of the largest and most regal birds in our area. It often stands motionless as it surveys the calm waters, its graceful lines blending naturally with the grasses and cattails of wetlands. All herons have specialized vertebrae that enable the neck to fold back over itself. The S-shaped neck, seen in flight, identifies all members of this wading family.

Hunting herons space themselves out evenly in favorite hunting spots, and they will strike out suddenly at prey below the water's surface. In flight, their lazy wing beats slowly but effortlessly carry them up to their nests. These herons nest communally high in trees, building bulky stick nests that are easily seen in Kensington Metropark. The shallows of Metro Beach Metropark, Lake Erie Metropark and Pointe Mouillee produce good views of this bird's unsurpassed elegance.

Similar Species: Great Egret (p. 22) has a similar build but is all white.

Quick I.D.: very large heron; eagle-sized wingspan; sexes similar; gray-blue plumage; long, dagger-like, yellow bill. *In flight:* head folded back; legs held straight back.
Size: 48–52 in.

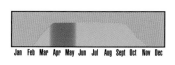

Jan Feb Mar Apr May Jun Jul Aug Sept Oct Nov Dec

Great Egret
Ardea alba

The silky silhouette of the Great Egret graces marshes in the Detroit area as it stalks the shallows for fish, amphibians and sometimes small birds and mammals. The diligence and patience it displays while hunting contrasts with its lightning-quick, spearing thrusts. At dusk, these ghostly birds trace their way back to their communal nesting and roosting sites, which are usually in areas isolated from humans. Although nesting activities are private affairs, there are usually a few of these majestic birds foraging in Lake Erie Metropark and Pointe Mouillee through the summer.

In spring, the Great Egret's form is enhanced by the presence of 'nuptial plumes' that flare from its lower neck. Early in the 20th century, these feathers were so coveted as fashion accessories that one ounce of feathers was worth more than an ounce of gold. Regrettably, Great Egret populations were decimated before legislation was enacted to protect them; we are seeing the triumphant return of these most exquisite birds in our area.

Similar Species: Great Blue Heron (p. 21) is gray-blue overall.

breeding

Quick I.D.: large heron; sexes similar; all-white plumage; long, yellow bill; black legs and feet. *Breeding:* long white plumes from back and base of neck; green lore.
Size: 37–40 in.

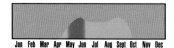

Jan Feb Mar Apr May Jun Jul Aug Sept Oct Nov Dec

Green Heron
Butorides virescens

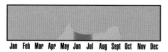

This crow-sized heron is far less conspicuous than its Great Blue cousin. The Green Heron prefers to hunt for frogs and small fish in shallow, weedy wetlands, where it is often seen perched just above the water's surface. By searching the shallow, shady, overgrown wetlands edges around Fairlane Lake at the University of Michigan–Dearborn, Detroit birders can sometimes get a prolonged view of this otherwise reclusive bird.

The Green Heron often uses all of its tiny stature to hunt over a favorite site. With its bright yellow feet clasping a branch or reed, this small heron stretches nearly horizontally over the water, its pose rigid and unchanging, until a fish swims into range. Like a taut bowstring, the tension mounts until the heron chooses to fire. Lunging its entire body at its prey, the heron is often soaked to the shoulders.

Similar Species: American Bittern is larger, is heavily streaked and lacks any green color.

Quick I.D.: crow-sized; sexes similar; small, stubby heron; short legs; glossy green back; chestnut throat; dark cap. *Breeding male:* orange legs. *Immature:* less colorful, with more streaking.
Size: 18–21 in.

Jan Feb Mar Apr May Jun Jul Aug Sept Oct Nov Dec

Sora

Porzana carolina

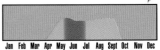

Skulking around freshwater marshes in the Detroit area is the seldom-seen Sora. Although this rail arrives in good numbers in spring, it is not a species that can be encountered with any predictability. Visual meetings with the Sora in Detroit arise unexpectedly, usually when birdwatchers are out in a wetland searching for less reclusive species. Its loud call—*So-ra So-ra!*, followed by a descending whinny—can still be heard at many area marshes.

Urban sprawl and agricultural expansion have come at the expense of many Detroit birds. The Sora's marshland habitat is often thought to be unproductive by human standards, but these shallow, nutrient-rich wetlands host a bounty of wildlife. With the growing legion of birdwatchers and nature lovers, societal values are finally shifting toward a holistic understanding of our natural communities.

Similar Species: Virginia Rail has a long, reddish, downcurved bill.

breeding

Jan Feb Mar Apr May Jun Jul Aug Sept Oct Nov Dec

Quick I.D.: robin-sized; sexes similar; short, yellow bill; front of face is black; gray neck and breast; long, greenish legs.
Size: 8–10 in.

American Coot
Fulica americana

The American Coot is a curious mix of comedy and confusion: it seems to have been made up of bits and pieces leftover from other birds. It has the lobed toes of a grebe, the bill of a chicken and the body shape and swimming habits of a duck, but it is not remotely related to any of these species: its closest cousins are rails and cranes. American Coots dabble and dive in water and forage on land, and they eat both plant and animal matter. They can be found in a few freshwater marshes in the Detroit area.

These loud, grouchy birds are usually seen chugging along in wetlands, frequently entering into short-lived disputes with other coots. American Coots appear comical while they swim: their heads bob in time with their paddling feet, and as a coot's swimming speed increases, so does the back-and-forth motion of its head. At peak speed, this motion seems to disorient the coot, so it prefers to run, flap and splash to the other side of the wetland.

Similar Species: All ducks and grebes generally lack the uniform black color and the all-white bill. Pied-billed Grebe (p. 19) is brown.

Quick I.D.: smaller than a duck; sexes similar; black body; white bill; red forehead shield; short tail; long legs; lobed feet; white undertail coverts.
Size: 14–16 in.

Jan Feb Mar Apr May Jun Jul Aug Sept Oct Nov Dec

Mute Swan
Cygnus olor

Gracing waters throughout the Metro Detroit area, the Mute Swan looks and acts like a movie star. Its beauty and silken wing plumes, with the warm accents of black and orange on its head, and its romantic composure grant this bird a regal stature. The Mute Swan has a very nasty side, however, pecking and pinching at any individual, be it bird or human, that dares to challenge its space.

This Eurasian native was introduced to Michigan in 1919 to grace estates and city parks. It first bred in the 1920s, and it has since established itself in many areas throughout the state. A non-migrant, the Mute Swan appears to thrive throughout the summer and it endures our winters in the open waters of Lake St. Clair and the Detroit River. Like so many of our introduced animals, the Mute Swan can displace certain native Michigan species and over-graze vegetation locally.

Similar Species: Tundra Swan has an all-black bill that lacks a knob, and it holds its neck straighter.

Jan Feb Mar Apr May Jun Jul Aug Sept Oct Nov Dec

Quick I.D.: larger than a goose; sexes similar; all-white body; orange or pink bill with black knob at base; black feet; thick neck; often swims with wings slightly raised. *Immature:* grayish-brownish body; all dark bill.
Size: 52–60 in. (male slightly larger).

Canada Goose
Branta canadensis

Most flocks of Canada Geese in city parks and golf courses show little concern for their human neighbors. These urban geese seem to think nothing of creating a traffic jam, blocking a fairway or dining on a lawn. Their love of manicured parks and gardens and the lack of predators have created somewhat of a population explosion in parts of the Detroit area.

Breeding pairs of Canada Geese are regal in appearance, and their loyalty is legendary. They mate for life, and not only will a widowed goose occasionally remain unpaired for the rest of its life, it's common for a mate to stay at the side of a fallen partner.

Similar Species: None.

Quick I.D.: large goose; sexes similar; white cheek; black head and neck; brown body; white undertail coverts.
Size: 35–42 in.

Jan Feb Mar Apr May Jun Jul Aug Sept Oct Nov Dec

Wood Duck
Aix sponsa

Only days old, small Wood Duck ducklings are lured out of the only world they have known by their pleading mother. Most ducklings leave the nest at this age, but young Wood Ducks require more coaxing than most—their nest is an old woodpecker hole high in a tree. With a faith-filled leap, the cottonball ducklings tumble to the ground, often bouncing on impact. When all the siblings have leapt into the waiting world, they follow their mother through the dense underbrush to the nearest water.

Many of the old, rotten, hollow trees that provided excellent nesting sites for Wood Ducks have been removed from the Detroit area. As a result, more and more young Wood Ducks are beginning life by tumbling out of human-made nest boxes. The Wood Ducks are provided with a secure nest site in which to incubate their eggs, while landowners have the honor of housing North America's most handsome duck. The male Wood Duck is one of the most colorful birds in North America. No other duck can match its much celebrated, iridescent, colorful and intricate plumage.

Similar Species: Male is very distinctive. Female is the only duck with a bold white eye ring and a short crest.

Jan Feb Mar Apr May Jun Jul Aug Sept Oct Nov Dec

Quick I.D.: small duck. *Male:* glossy green head; crest slicked back from crown; white chin and throat; chestnut breast spotted white; white shoulder slash; golden sides; dark back and hindquarters. *Female:* white 'teardrop' eye patch; mottled brown breast streaked white; brown-gray upperparts; white belly.
Size: 18–20 in.

Mallard
Anas platyrhynchos

The Mallard is the classic duck of inland marshes—the male's iridescent green head and chestnut breast are symbolic of wetland habitat. This large duck is commonly seen feeding in city parks, small lakes and shallow bays. With their legs positioned under the middle part of their bodies, Mallards walk easily, and they can spring straight out of water without a running start.

Mallards are the most common duck in North America (and the Northern Hemisphere), and they are easily seen year-round in Detroit. During winter, flocks of Mallards are seen in open water or grazing along shorelines. Because several species often band together in these loose flocks, birdwatchers habitually scan these groups to test their identification skills. Mallards (like all ducks) molt several times a year, so remember that the distinctive green head of the male Mallard occasionally loses its green pizzazz.

Similar Species: Female resembles many other female dabbling ducks, but look for the blue speculum, bordered by white on both sides, and her close association with the distinctive male. Male Northern Shoveler (p. 31) has a green head, white breast and chestnut flanks.

Quick I.D.: large duck; bright orange feet; blue speculum bordered by white.
Male: iridescent green head; bright yellow bill; chestnut breast; white flanks.
Female: mottled brown; bright orange bill marked with black.
Size: 22–26 in.

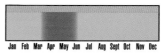

Blue-winged Teal
Anas discors

The male Blue-winged Teal has a thin, white crescent on his cheek and a steel blue head to match his inner wing patches. These small ducks are extremely swift flyers, which frustrates their many predators. Their sleek design and rapid wing beats enable teals to swerve, even at great speeds, and also give these small ducks the accuracy to make pinpoint landings.

Unlike many of the larger dabblers, which overwinter in the United States, teals migrate to Central and South America. For this reason, the Blue-winged Teal is often the last duck to arrive in Detroit during spring and the first to leave in fall, usually by the end of September.

Similar Species: Female is easily confused with other female ducks.

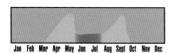

Jan Feb Mar Apr May Jun Jul Aug Sept Oct Nov Dec

Quick I.D.: very small duck; blue speculum. *Male:* steel blue head; white crescent on cheek. *Female:* small, plain; yellow-orange legs; gray bill.
Size: 14–16 in.

Northern Shoveler
Anas clypeata

The Northern Shoveler's shovel-like bill stands out among dabbling ducks—the species name, *clypeata*, is Latin for 'furnished with a shield.' The comb-like structures along the bill's edges and its broad, flat shape allow the shoveler to strain small plants and invertebrates from the water's surface or from muddy substrates.

Very few Northern Shovelers breed in the Detroit area; most breed farther west, and they can be seen here during their spring and fall migrations.

Many novice birders become interested in birds because they realize the great variety of ducks in their city parks. Some ducks, like the Northern Shoveler, are dabblers, which prefer shallow water, are not opposed to roaming around on land and can lift straight off the water like a helicopter. Many of the ducks that are found on large lakes in the Detroit area are divers. They can be seen running across the water to gain enough speed for flight. Separating the divers from the dabblers is a first step into the wondrous world of waterfowl.

Similar Species: Mallard (p. 29) and all other dabbling ducks lack the combination of a large bill, a white breast and chestnut sides.

Quick I.D.: mid-sized duck; large bill (longer than head width). *Male:* green head; white breast; chestnut sides. *Female:* mottled brown overall.
Size: 18–20 in.

Jan Feb Mar Apr May Jun Jul Aug Sept Oct Nov Dec

Gadwall
Anas strepera

Among the flocks of ducks floating offshore of Belle Isle during migration, you might find our most unassuming species of waterfowl, the Gadwall. At a quick glance, a male Gadwall can pass for a female Mallard, but this 'Plain Jane' of the duck world impresses many birdwatchers with its subtle beauty.

Gadwalls are built perfectly for dabbling, which they perform with the same teeter-totter expertise as Mallards. Gadwalls, however, are also frequently observed diving for their food. Although they are heavily built and are not as streamlined as most of the classic duck divers, Gadwalls show resourcefulness and adaptability in deep and shallow waters.

Similar Species: Female Mallard (p. 29) has a blue speculum. Female Green-winged Teal has a green speculum and is smaller.

Jan Feb Mar Apr May Jun Jul Aug Sept Oct Nov Dec

Quick I.D.: mid-sized duck; black-and-white wing patch (often seen in resting birds); white belly. *Male:* mostly gray; black hindquarters. *Female:* mottled brown.
Size: 19–21 in.

American Wigeon
Anas americana

During their spring and fall migrations, American Wigeons can easily be found and identified in marshes along the Detroit River and Lake St. Clair. Flocks of wigeons waddle across lawns and are regulars floating offshore on Lake Erie. The white top and gray sides of the male American Wigeon's head look somewhat like a balding scalp, while the nasal *wee-he-he-he!* calls sound remarkably like the squeaks of a squeezed rubber ducky.

The concentrated spring run north is generally less productive for birdwatchers than the return of the birds through the month of October, when hundreds of wigeons can be seen on the water, feeding and refueling for the continuation of their trip. Although they breed to the north and winter primarily on the Atlantic, a few American Wigeons occasionally spend the summer at Pointe Mouillee.

Similar Species: Green-winged Teal is smaller, has a white shoulder slash and has a rusty head with a green swipe.

Quick I.D.: mid-sized duck; cinnamon breast and flanks; white belly; gray bill with black tip; green speculum. *Male:* white forehead; green swipe running back from eye. *Female:* lacks distinct color on head.
Size: 18–21 in.

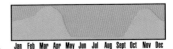

Jan Feb Mar Apr May Jun Jul Aug Sept Oct Nov Dec

Canvasback
Aythya valisineria

During migration and in winter, hundreds of these white-backed ducks can be seen on Lake St. Clair and the Detroit River, majestically swimming in open waters with their bills held high. Canvasbacks are ducks of the deep freshwater, and they acquire their vegetarian diet in well-spaced dives. Birders can easily identify the stately Canvasback at a distance. Its distinctive profile results from the apparent lack of a forehead. The dark bill appears to run straight up to the top of the bird's head, giving the Canvasback sleek, hydrodynamic-looking contours.

The Redhead is a closely related duck that is very similar in appearance. Like the male Canvasback, the male Redhead's head is—you guessed it—red, but its back is gray. Also, the Redhead has a noticeable forehead, just like it is wearing a ball cap.

Similar Species: Lesser Scaup (p. 35) lacks the chestnut head and the sloping forehead. Redhead lacks the sloping forehead and has a black-tipped, gray bill and a darker back.

Quick I.D.: mid-sized duck; sloping, black bill and forehead. *Male:* canvas white back; chestnut head; black breast and hindquarters. *Female:* brown head and neck; lighter body.
Size: 19–22 in.

Lesser Scaup
Aythya affinis

The Lesser Scaup is the Oreo cookie of the duck world—black at both ends and white in the middle. It is a diving duck that prefers deep, open water, and it is common on lakes, harbors and lagoons. As a result of its diving adaptations, the Lesser Scaup is clumsy on land and during take-off, but it gains dignity when it takes to the water. For the best views, visit Belle Isle and Lake Erie Metropark.

Because of Detroit's location on the Great Lakes, diving ducks are the most abundant ducks in our area, even though the dabblers are often the most frequently encountered. Diving ducks have smaller wings, which helps them dive underwater but makes for difficult take-offs and landings. When a duck scoots across the water in an attempt to get airborne, even a first-time birder can tell it's a diver. Divers' legs are placed well back on their bodies—an advantage for underwater swimming—so in order for diving ducks to stand, they must raise their heavy front ends high to maintain balance.

Similar Species: Greater Scaup has a green tinge to its more rounded head and a long white stripe on the trailing edge of its wing (seen in flight). Ring-necked Duck has a white breast slash and a black back.

Quick I.D.: small duck; peaked head.
Male: dark head with hints of purple; black breast and hindquarters; dirty white sides; grayish back; blue-gray bill; no white breast slash. *Female:* dark brown; well-defined white patch at base of bill.
Size: 15–17 in.

Jan Feb Mar Apr May Jun Jul Aug Sept Oct Nov Dec

Common Goldeneye
Bucephala clangula

Although Common Goldeneyes don't breed in the Detroit area, they are locally common from late fall right up to their spring migration. Their courtship antics, staged off Belle Isle and on Lake St. Clair from winter through spring, reinforce a pair's bond prior to their migration to northern woodland lakes.

The courtship display of this widespread duck is one of nature's best slapstick routines. The spry male goldeneye rapidly arches his large green head back until his bill points skyward, producing a seemingly painful *kraaaagh!* Completely unaffected by this chiropractic wonder, he repeatedly performs this ritual to mainly disinterested females. The male continually escalates his spring performance, creating a comedic scene that is most appreciated by birdwatchers.

Similar Species: Hooded Merganser and Bufflehead (p. 37) lack the round, white face patch.

Quick I.D.: mid-sized duck. *Male:* large, dark green to black head; round, white cheek patch; white body; black back streaked with white. *Female:* chocolate-brown hood; sandy-colored body.
Size: 17–19 in.

Jan Feb Mar Apr May Jun Jul Aug Sept Oct Nov Dec

Bufflehead
Bucephala albeola

The small, 'baby-faced' Bufflehead is perhaps the 'cutest' of Detroit's ducks: its simple plumage and rotund physique bring to mind a child's stuffed toy. During winter, a few of these charming birds are found on Lake St. Clair, Lake Erie and the Detroit River.

Because ducks spend most of their lives dripping with water, preening is an important behavior. At the base of the tail of most birds lies the preen (uropygial) gland, which secretes a viscous liquid that inhibits bacterial growth and waterproofs and conditions the feathers. After gently squeezing the preen gland with its bill, a bird can spread the secretion methodically over most of its body, an essential practice to revitalize precious feathers. Because sun and wind damage feathers, it is understandable that birds spend so much time preening and conditioning their feathers.

Similar Species: Male Common Goldeneye (p. 36) is larger and lacks the white, unbordered triangle behind the eye.

Quick I.D.: tiny duck; round body.
Male: white triangle on back of dark head; white body; dark back. *Female:* dirty brown; small white cheek patch.
Size: 13–15 in.

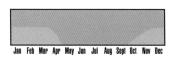

Jan Feb Mar Apr May Jun Jul Aug Sept Oct Nov Dec

Common Merganser
Mergus merganser

Looking like a large jumbo jet taking off, the Common Merganser runs along the surface of the water, beating its heavy wings, until it has sufficient speed for lift-off. Once in the air, our largest duck looks compressed and arrow-like as it flies strongly in low, straight lines.

Mergansers are lean and powerful waterfowl designed for the underwater pursuit of fish. Unlike the bills of other fish-eating birds, a merganser's bill is saw-like, serrated to ensure that its squirmy, slimy prey does not escape.

Common Mergansers are cavity nesters, breeding wherever there are suitable lakes and trees, and they are often seen on rivers. In Detroit, Common Mergansers are seen during migration and winter, when these large ducks congregate in rafts in areas of open water.

Similar Species: Common Loon (p. 18) has a straight, dark bill and darker sides. Red-breasted Merganser (p. 39) lacks the white breast and sides.

Quick I.D.: goose-sized. *Male:* well-defined, dark green hood; white body; brilliant orange bill and feet; black spinal streak. *Female:* rusty hood; clean white throat; gray body.
Size: 23–26 in.

Jan Feb Mar Apr May Jun Jul Aug Sept Oct Nov Dec

Red-breasted Merganser
Mergus serrator

During spring, Red-breasted Mergansers congregate near the shores of Lake St. Clair and along the Detroit River, initiating their courting rituals prior to their final push north. Males, with their punk-like, slicked crests, ride the waters while lowering their necks under the surface. With their mid-points submerged, these ducks stare eerily with their wild red eyes, evaluating the female's response to their actions.

Large, gregarious flocks of Red-breasted Mergansers visit the Great Lakes during migration. However, unlike their relative, the Common Merganser, they tend to retreat to coastal waters for the winter. During their stay in our area, their quick 'fly bys' and flashing, white inner wing patches are common features off Belle Isle.

Similar Species: Male Common Merganser (p. 38) lacks the red breast and has white underparts, and the female has a well-defined, reddish-brown hood. Common Loon (p. 18) and other large ducks lack the combination of a green head, an orange bill, orange feet and a red breast.

Quick I.D.: large duck; gray body.
Male: well-defined, dark green hood; punk-like crest; spotted, red breast; white collar; brilliant orange bill and feet; black spinal streak. *Female:* rusty hood blending into white chest.
Size: 21–25 in.

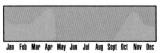

Jan Feb Mar Apr May Jun Jul Aug Sept Oct Nov Dec

Turkey Vulture
Cathartes aura

Soaring effortlessly above Lake Erie Metropark, Turkey Vultures ride rising thermals during their October migratory flights. They seldom need to flap their silver-lined wings, and they rock gently from side to side as they carefully scan fields and shorelines for carcasses. Even at great distances, this bare-headed bird can be identified by the way it tends to hold its wings upward in a shallow 'V.'

The Turkey Vulture feeds entirely on carrion, which it can sometimes detect by scent alone. Its head is featherless, which is an adaptation to staying clean and parasite-free while it digs around inside carcasses. This king of the scavengers has a well-known habit of regurgitating its rotting meal at intruders to its nest. This action might be a defense mechanism: it allows Turkey Vultures to reduce their weight for a quicker take-off, and the smell helps young vultures repel would-be predators.

Similar Species: Hawks, eagles and Osprey all have large, feathered heads and tend to hold their wings flatter in flight, not in a shallow 'V.'

Quick I.D.: larger than a hawk; sexes similar; all black; small, red head.
In flight: wings held in shallow 'V'; silver-gray flight feathers; dark wing linings; rocks from side to side.
Size: 27–30 in.

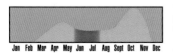

Jan Feb Mar Apr May Jun Jul Aug Sept Oct Nov Dec

Sharp-shinned Hawk
Accipiter striatus

If songbirds dream, the Sharp-shinned Hawk is sure to be the source of their nightmares. These raptors pursue small birds through forests, maneuvering around limbs and branches in the hope of acquiring prey. Sharp-shinned Hawks prey on many birds, with small songbirds and the occasional woodpecker being the most numerous prey items.

These small hawks are easy to find at Lake Erie Metropark when they pass through our area in September and October. During the winter months, many of Detroit's wooded neighborhoods have a resident 'Sharpie' eager to catch unwary finches, sparrows and starlings. Backyard feeders tend to concentrate sparrows and finches, so they are attractive foraging areas for this small hawk. A sudden eruption of songbirds off the feeder and a few feathers floating on the wind are often the signs of a sudden, successful Sharp-shinned attack.

Similar Species: Cooper's Hawk is larger, and its tail is rounded and has a wide terminal band. Merlin has pointed wings and rapid wing beats, and it lacks the red chest barring.

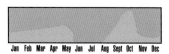

Quick I.D.: pigeon-sized; sexes similar; short, round wings; long tail. *Adult:* blue-gray back; red barring on underparts; red eyes. *In flight:* flap-and-glide flier; barred tail is straight at end. *Immature:* brown overall; vertical, brown streaks on chest; yellow eyes.
Size: 12–14 in. (female larger).

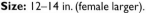

Jan Feb Mar Apr May Jun Jul Aug Sept Oct Nov Dec

Broad-winged Hawk
Buteo platypterus

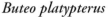

Sighting this mid-sized hawk is a hit-and-miss affair. Broad-winged Hawks are fairly secretive in their wooded breeding habitat, and many summers can pass without one being seen. During their migrations, however, certain areas, such as Lake Erie Metropark, can produce tens of thousands in a single day! The peak, which lasts only three or four days, usually occurs between September 10 and September 20 each year.

Hawks' heavy wings are not designed for continual flapping flight, so these raptors seek out areas with updrafts that reduce their need to flap. The Great Lakes are daunting to Broad-winged Hawks, which prefer to skirt around the edges, funneling through areas that provide welcome updrafts. The rising air currents help them gain elevation before they launch across a stretch of stagnant, heavy air.

Similar Species: Red-tailed Hawk (p. 43) has a solid red tail. Sharp-shinned Hawk (p. 41) has a long, narrow tail. Rough-legged Hawk is a winter visitor. Red-shouldered Hawk has narrow, white bands on its black tail and red shoulders.

Jan Feb Mar Apr May Jun Jul Aug Sept Oct Nov Dec

Quick I.D.: smaller than a crow; sexes similar. *Adult:* wide white bands on black, fan-like tail; russet barring on chest; rounded wings.
Size: 15–17 in.

Red-tailed Hawk
Buteo jamaicensis

With its fierce facial expression and untidy feathers, the Red-tailed Hawk looks as though it has been suddenly and rudely awakened. Its characteristic scream further suggests that the Red-tailed Hawk is a bird best avoided. You would think other birds would treat this large raptor with more respect, but the Red-tailed Hawk is constantly being harassed by crows, jays and blackbirds.

It isn't until this hawk is two or three years old that its tail becomes brick red. The dark head, black 'belt' around its midsection and the dark leading edge to its wings are better field marks because they're seen in most Red-tails.

Wherever highways pass through open country, it's hard not to spot a Red-tail perched on a post or soaring lazily overhead.

Similar Species: Sharp-shinned Hawk (p. 41) and Cooper's Hawk are smaller and have long tails. Broad-winged Hawk (p. 42) has a boldly banded tail. Northern Harrier has a white rump and a long tail.

Quick I.D.: large hawk; sexes similar; brick-red tail (adult only); brown head; variable brown speckled belt; light flight feathers; dark wing lining and leading edge.
Size: 20–24 in.

Jan Feb Mar Apr May Jun Jul Aug Sept Oct Nov Dec

American Kestrel
Falco sparverius

This small, noisy falcon is a common summer sight over much of the Detroit area. It has adapted well to urban life, and it is commonly seen perched on power lines, watching for unwary grasshoppers, birds and rodents. When not perched, American Kestrels can often be seen hovering above potential prey. American Kestrels might be encountered along many highways. These small falcons typically leave their powerline perches as vehicles approach.

All falcons are skilled hunters, and they have a unique, tooth-like projection on their hooked bills that can quickly crush the necks of small prey. The American Kestrel's species name, *sparverius*, is Latin for 'pertaining to sparrows,' an occasional prey item.

American Kestrels often build their nests in abandoned woodpecker cavities. Conservationists have recently discovered that kestrels will use nest boxes when natural cavities are unavailable, which should ensure that these active predators remain common throughout the Detroit area.

Similar Species: Sharp-shinned Hawk (p. 41) and Cooper's Hawk have short, rounder wings. Merlin is larger, has a banded tail and has boldly streaked underparts.

Quick I.D.: smaller than a jay; long, pointed wings; long tail; two vertical, black stripes on each side of face; spotted breast; hooked bill. *In flight:* rapid wing beat. *Male:* blue wings; russet back; colorful head. *Female:* russet back and wings.
Size: 8–9 in.

Jan Feb Mar Apr May Jun Jul Aug Sept Oct Nov Dec

Ruffed Grouse
Bonasa umbellus

Hikers are often amazed by the Ruffed Grouse. It is not this bird's voice, plumage or spectacular flights that draw attention to it, but rather its habit of doing nothing. It is not out of stupidity that Ruffed Grouse freeze, remaining motionless despite the advances of curious onlookers. In reality, this adaptation serves grouse well, because their plumage provides the birds with effective camouflage—for every grouse that is seen, many more are probably overlooked. In the majority of grouse-human interactions, it is likely the birds that smugly marvel at the dull-sensed passersby.

Ruffed Grouse can be encountered year-round in wooded areas in Oakland County, but it is only in spring that their deep courting sounds are heard. The muffled sounds are so deep that they are often felt before they are heard. To produce the sound, males drum their wings in accelerating beats. Although it may appear that the birds strike their breasts, all they beat is the air.

Similar Species: Female Ring-necked Pheasant has a long, unbanded, pointed tail, lacks the crest and has unfeathered legs.

♂

gray phase

Quick I.D.: chicken-like; sexes similar; mottled grayish-brown or reddish-brown (two color phases); multi-banded tail; black shoulder patch (not always evident); crest raised only in alarm and arousal.
Size: 16–18 in.

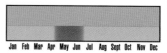

Jan Feb Mar Apr May Jun Jul Aug Sept Oct Nov Dec

Northern Bobwhite
Colinus virginianus

From a dense brush pile or hedgerow in early spring, bursts a rising *Bob-white!* call. Although their calls give away their identity, the scurrying birds often refuse to be seen; they stubbornly remain hidden in protective cover. As the Midwest's only native quail, the Northern Bobwhite alone displays this group's unusual behaviors to Detroit-area naturalists.

Outside of the brief spring courtship season, Northern Bobwhites gather together in groups of typically about dozen birds. Known as 'coveys,' these marauding bands forage widely for seeds, leaves and insects on farmlands in our area.

Detroit is near the northern limit of this quail's natural range, and our harsh winters can be quite hard on these small birds. To retain body heat, coveys roost together on the ground in circles, with their tails pointing inward and their heads pointing out. This unusual behavior is not only effective in sharing communal warmth; it also ensures that each bird has a clear take-off path should a threat arise.

Similar Species: None.

Quick I.D.: larger than a robin; plump reddish brown body; short tail; chestnut streaks on flanks. *Male:* bold, black-and-white facial pattern; white throat. *Female:* black-and-buff facial pattern; buff throat.
Size: 10 in.

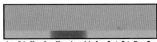

Jan Feb Mar Apr May Jun Jul Aug Sept Oct Nov Dec

Killdeer
Charadrius vociferus

The Killdeer is the most widespread shorebird in the Detroit area. It nests on gravelly shorelines, utility rights-of-way, lawns, pastures and occasionally on gravel roofs and parking lots within cities. Its name is a paraphrase of its distinctive, loud call—*kill-dee kill-dee kill-deer!*

The Killdeer's response to predators relies on deception and good acting skills. To divert a predator's attention away from a nest or a brood of young, an adult Killdeer (like many shorebirds) will flop around to feign an injury (usually a broken wing). Once the Killdeer has the attention of the fox, crow or gull, it leads the predator away from the vulnerable nest. After it reaches a safe distance, the adult Killdeer is suddenly 'healed' and flies off, leaving the predator without a meal.

Similar Species: Semipalmated Plover has only one chest band, is smaller and is found mostly on mudflats.

Quick I.D.: robin-sized; sexes similar; two black bands across breast; brown back; russet rump; long legs; white underparts.
Size: 9–11 in.

Jan Feb Mar Apr May Jun Jul Aug Sept Oct Nov Dec

Lesser Yellowlegs
Tringa flavipes

breeding

On a spring walk along the shores of Lake Erie Metropark or Pointe Mouillee, you can see a few different sandpipers. The Lesser Yellowlegs prefers shallow pools where it can peck for small invertebrates, but it might venture belly-deep into the water to pursue prey. Occasionally, a yellowlegs can be seen hopping along on one leg, with the other one tucked up in the body feathers to reduce heat loss.

Many birders enjoy the challenge of distinguishing the Lesser Yellowlegs from the Greater Yellowlegs. The Greater, which is less numerous in our area (but don't let that bias your identification), has a relatively longer, heavier bill that is slightly upturned—so slightly that you notice it one moment and not the next. Generally, the Lesser's call is a *tew! tew!*, and the Greater's is a *tew! tew! tew!* Many experienced birders will name them at a glance, but others are satisfied with writing 'unidentified yellowlegs' in their field notes.

Similar Species: Greater Yellowlegs is larger and has a longer, upturned bill. Stilt Sandpiper has a droopy bill and a more pronounced eyebrow.

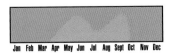

Jan Feb Mar Apr May Jun Jul Aug Sept Oct Nov Dec

Quick I.D.: pigeon-sized; sexes similar; long, bright yellow legs; finely streaked gray body; bill shorter than head width.
Size: 9–11 in.

Solitary Sandpiper
Tringa solitaria

True to its name, the Solitary Sandpiper is frequently seen alone or in small groups along the shores of inland lakes and Lake Erie. This antisocial behaviour is fairly unusual among migrating shorebirds, but the Solitary Sandpiper's habit of bobbing its body like a Latin dancer is actually its most striking feature.

Solitary Sandpipers stalk shorelines, picking up aquatic invertebrates, such as waterboatmen and damselfly nymphs. Unlike most other shorebirds, these northern breeders have been known to cleverly stir the water with a foot to spook out prey.

No other shorebird has such an unusual nesting site—up a tree! The Solitary Sandpiper's nesting strategy remained undiscovered for many years, because early ornithologists never thought to look for this bird's nests in abandoned songbird nests in trees. Its voice is a high, thin *peet-wheet!* or *wheet wheet wheet!* during summer.

Similar Species: Lesser Yellowlegs (p. 48) has bright yellow legs and no eye ring. Spotted Sandpiper (p. 49) has an incomplete eye ring, a very spotted breast and an orange, black-tipped bill.

breeding

Quick I.D.: robin-sized; sexes similar; white eye ring; short green legs; brown-gray spotted back; white lore; brown-gray head; neck and breast have fine white streaks; dark uppertail with black and white barring on sides.
Size: 8–9 in.

Jan Feb Mar Apr May Jun Jul Aug Sept Oct Nov Dec

Spotted Sandpiper
Actitis macularia

breeding

This common shorebird of lakes and rivers has a most uncommon mating strategy. In a reversal of the gender roles of most birds, female Spotted Sandpipers compete in the spring for the males. After the nest is built and the eggs are laid, the female leaves to find another mate, while the first male is left to incubate the eggs. This behavior can be repeated two or more times before the female settles down with one male to raise her last brood of chicks. Spotted Sandpipers nest in the Detroit area, and they are frequently encountered during the migratory months along undisturbed shores and rocky piers.

The Spotted Sandpiper is readily identified by its arthritic-looking, stiff-winged flight low over water. Its peppy call—*eat-wheat wheat-wheat-wheat*—bursts from startled birds as they retreat from shoreline disturbances. Spotted Sandpipers constantly teeter and bob when they are not in flight, which makes them easy to identify.

Similar Species: Killdeer (p. 47) has dark throat bands. Solitary Sandpiper (p. 49) has an eye ring and lacks the prominent breast spots. Lesser Yellowlegs (p. 48) has longer legs.

Jan Feb Mar Apr May Jun Jul Aug Sept Oct Nov Dec

Quick I.D.: smaller than a robin; often teeters and bobs; yellow legs.
Breeding: spotted breast; olive-gray back; yellow bill tipped with black. *Female:* spots more pronounced.
Size: 7–8 in.

Sanderling
Calidris alba

A spring or fall stroll at Pointe Mouillee or Metro Beach Metropark is often punctuated by the sight of these tiny runners, which appear to enjoy nothing more than playing in the surf. Sanderlings are characteristically seen chasing and retreating from the rolling waves, never getting caught in the charging water. Only the Sanderling commonly forages in this manner, plucking at the exposed invertebrates stirred up by the wave action. Without waves to chase along calm shorelines, Sanderlings unenthusiastically probe into wet soil in much the same fashion as many other sandpipers.

This sandpiper is one of the world's most widespread birds. It breeds across the Arctic in Alaska, Canada and Russia, and it spends the winter running up and down sandy shorelines in North America, South America, Asia, Africa and Australia.

Similar Species: Least Sandpiper (p. 52) is smaller and darker. Dunlin (p. 54) is darker and has a downcurved bill.

non-breeding

Quick I.D.: smaller than a robin; straight, black bill; dark legs. *Breeding:* rusty head and breast. *Non-breeding:* white underparts; grayish-white upperparts; black shoulder patch (sometimes concealed).
Size: 7¹/₂–8¹/₂ in.

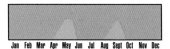

Jan Feb Mar Apr May Jun Jul Aug Sept Oct Nov Dec

Least Sandpiper
Calidris minutilla

non-breeding

The Least Sandpiper is the smallest of our shorebirds, but its size is not a deterrent to its migratory feats. Like most other 'peeps'—a term used to group the sometimes difficult to identify *Calidris* sandpipers—the Least Sandpipers passing through Detroit migrate to the Arctic to breed.

Groups of these tiny birds can be spotted against mudflats and lakeshores throughout our area. Their plumage matches perfectly with their preferred habitat, and it is usually their rapid movements that reveal these diminutive sprinters. Least Sandpipers tenaciously peck the moist substrate with their dexterous bills, eating mosquitoes, beach fleas, amphipods and other aquatic invertebrates.

Similar Species: Pectoral Sandpiper (p. 53) is larger and has a well-defined pectoral border. Other 'peeps' tend to have dark legs and are generally larger.

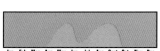

Jan Feb Mar Apr May Jun Jul Aug Sept Oct Nov Dec

Quick I.D.: sparrow-sized; sexes similar; black bill; yellow legs; dark, mottled back; buff-brown breast, head and nape; light breast streaking. *Immature:* like an adult, but with faintly streaked breast.
Size: 5–6 in.

Pectoral Sandpiper
Calidris melanotos

Pectoral Sandpipers foraging on the shorelines at Pointe Mouillee tie the Detroit area ecologically into an international mosaic: the sandpipers that dot our shorelines in April require the invertebrates in Michigan's mud to fuel up for the completion of their migration to the arctic tundra.

The Pectoral Sandpiper is one of the few sandpiper species that shows sexual dimorphism: the females are only two-thirds the size of the males. The common name 'pectoral' refers to the location of the male's prominent air sacs. When a predator approaches, this sandpiper frequently inflates the air sacks in its neck in alarm, raising its feathers. The males also use these sacs as part of their courtship ritual, inflating them passionately. Although the name refers to these air sacs, it is also a convenient memory aid: the Pectoral Sandpiper has an abrupt bib across its upper chest.

Similar Species: Other 'peeps' lack the well-defined light belly and densely streaked pectoral region.

non-breeding

Quick I.D.: smaller than a robin; sexes similar; moderately long, yellow legs; brown breast streaks contrast with light belly and undertail coverts; black, slightly downcurved bill; mottled upperparts; dark crown; wing tips extend beyond tail.
Size: 9 in.

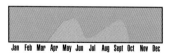

Jan Feb Mar Apr May Jun Jul Aug Sept Oct Nov Dec

Dunlin
Calidris alpina

These small, plump shorebirds are not remarkable in and of themselves, but their flocks are spectacular. Outside the breeding season, Dunlins are communal creatures, and the magic of this species is in a cloud of hundreds of individuals flying wingtip to wingtip, instantaneously changing course as one. These hypnotic flights, flashing alternating shades of white and black, are occasionally seen as Dunlins migrate along Lake St. Clair's shores. Although the flocks move about continuously around Detroit-area shorelines, Pointe Mouillee often hosts hundreds of Dunlins during migration. These tight flocks are generally more exclusive than many other shorebird troupes: few species mix with groups of Dunlins.

The Dunlin, like most other shorebirds, nests on the arctic tundra and winters on the coasts of North America, Europe and Asia. It was originally called the 'Dunling' (meaning 'a small brown bird'), but for unknown reasons the 'g' was later dropped.

Similar Species: Least Sandpiper (p. 52) is smaller. Sanderling (p. 51) is paler and is usually seen running in the surf.

breeding

Quick I.D.: smaller than a robin; sexes similar; slightly downcurved bill; dark legs. *Breeding:* black belly; streaked underparts; rusty back. *Non-breeding:* pale gray underparts; grayish-brown upperparts
Size: 8–9 in.

Jan Feb Mar Apr May Jun Jul Aug Sept Oct Nov Dec

Common Snipe
Gallinago gallinago

Common Snipes have startled many walkers who stroll through Metro Beach Metropark marshes. These shorebirds are both secretive and well camouflaged, so few people notice them until the birds fly out suddenly from nearby grassy tussocks. As soon as snipes take to the air, they perform a series of quick zig-zags, an evasive maneuver designed to confuse predators. Snipes are seldom seen in large groups, and they are rarely encountered along open shorelines—their heavily streaked plumage is suited to grassy habitats.

This mystical 'winnowing' sound of courting Common Snipes is heard infrequently in the Detroit area because their breeding habitat has largely been destroyed. During spring evenings at Indian Springs Metropark, however, the accelerating sound, produced in flight by air passing through the spread tail feathers, can thrill perceptive observers.

Similar Species: All other shorebirds either have shorter bills or are not as heavily streaked. American Woodcock (p. 56) is chunkier, has a rich buff color and has bars on its head.

Quick I.D.: robin-sized; sexes similar; long, black-tipped bill; heavily streaked back; short neck; striped head; long legs.
Size: 10½–11½ in.

Jan Feb Mar Apr May Jun Jul Aug Sept Oct Nov Dec

American Woodcock
Scolopax minor

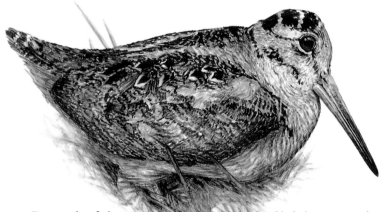

For much of the year, the American Woodcock's behavior matches its cryptic and unassuming attire. This well-camouflaged bird inhabits woods and thickets—its lifestyle does little to reveal itself to the outside world.

For a short month each spring, male woodcocks explode into vanity at Oakwoods Metropark and Bald Mountain State Recreation Area. The courtship performance begins when the male selects a clearing in the woods, where he gives a plaintive *bjeeent!* that inspires him into an Elvis-like boogie. Since the woodcock's legs are short, he usually selects a stage that is free of thick vegetation that would block the females' views of his swinging strut. When he has sashayed sufficiently, he takes to the air to punctuate the show. Spiraling upward into the evening sky, he twitters increasingly toward the sky-dance climax. Upon hitting the peak of his ascent, the male woodcock relaxes and then plummets, uncontrolled, to the ground. Just before striking the ground, the woodcock pulls out of the crippled dive and alights on his dancing stage, where he resumes his breeding ballet. To attend this long-running musical, visit a moist woodland in April or May. Admission is free, the singing and dancing are well choreographed, and the performance is powerful.

Similar Species: Common Snipe (p. 55) has a striped head and back, and painted wings.

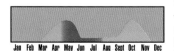

Jan Feb Mar Apr May Jun Jul Aug Sept Oct Nov Dec

Quick I.D.: jay-sized; sexes similar; chunky; very long bill; large eyes; rusty underparts. *In flight:* rounded wings.
Size: 10–12 in.

Bonaparte's Gull

Larus philadelphia

The scratchy little calls of Bonaparte's Gulls accompany these migrants as they forage along Detroit's shorelines. These gulls commonly feed on the water's surface, and they can often be seen resting atop concrete platforms. Bonaparte's Gulls pass through our area from the last two weeks of March through the first half of May. They are on their way north to breed in the northern boreal forest, where they nest, in most un–gull-like fashion, in spruce trees.

When they return to our area from October through December, Bonaparte's Gulls are more visible, but far less striking in appearance. After the summer breeding season, most Bonaparte's Gulls lose their distinctive black hoods, but they retain flashy white wing patches and a noticeable black spot behind the eye.

This gull was named not after the famed French emperor, but after his nephew, Charles Lucien Bonaparte, who brought recognition to his family's name through the practice of ornithology.

Similar Species: Common Tern (p. 60) and Forster's Tern have forked tails and lack the white wing flash.

non-breeding

Quick I.D.: small gull; sexes similar; black bill; dark eyes. *In flight:* wings flash white; wing tips have black outline. *Breeding:* black hood. *Non-breeding:* white head with dark ear spot.
Size: 12–14 in.

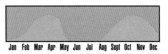

Jan Feb Mar Apr May Jun Jul Aug Sept Oct Nov Dec

Ring-billed Gull
Larus delawarensis

This widespread gull is extremely common in the Detroit area. It is slightly smaller than the Herring Gull and has a distinctive dark bill ring, for which it is well named. The Ring-billed Gull is a common sight in cities; it is frequently seen in parks or effortlessly soaring high overhead. The warm air rising from the concrete and asphalt are like elevators that dozens of gulls ride simultaneously, climbing until their sleek shapes vanish into the sky.

Although these gulls appear to be regular urbanites, like so many people in Detroit they commute daily into the city. From shoreline suburbs, gull traffic can be seen during early mornings, congested along skyways leading into town. Their daily activities involve squabbling with other greedy gulls for leftovers from fast food-restaurants and for food in open areas. Once a gull is nicely fed, it might break from its feeding duties by soaring high above the hectic pace of city life.

Similar Species: Herring Gull (p. 59) is larger, has pink legs and lacks the bill ring. Bonaparte's Gull (p. 57) is smaller and has a black head in spring and a white wing flash.

breeding

Quick I.D.: mid-sized gull; sexes similar.; black ring near bill tip; yellow bill and legs; dark gray wings; light eyes; black wing tips; small white spots on black primaries; white underparts. *Non-breeding:* white head and nape washed with brown. *First winter:* mottled grayish brown; gray back; blackish-brown primaries; brown band on tail.
Size: 18–20 in.

Jan Feb Mar Apr May Jun Jul Aug Sept Oct Nov Dec

Herring Gull
Larus argentatus

breeding

Many gulls come and go in Detroit, but the Herring Gull is a year-round resident in the Great Lakes region. This 'sea gull,' familiar to all, does not rightfully deserve that moniker, because the Herring Gulls seen in our area rarely venture to salt water. If it were to relinquish the title, however, it would likely be labeled with one even less desirable. Large flocks of this gull can be found in bays, lakes, garbage dumps, shorelines, city parks and agricultural fields. Herring Gulls are so widely distributed that they are sure to be sighted on just about any birding trip taken along the shores of Lake Erie, Lake St. Clair or the Detroit River.

Although it is often overlooked by even the most curious naturalist, the Herring Gull is an engineering marvel. Agile on land, an effortless flyer, wonderfully adaptive and with a stomach for anything digestible, the Herring Gull is perhaps the most widely distributed gull in North America.

Similar Species: Ring-billed Gull (p. 58) has yellow legs and a banded bill.

Quick I.D.: hawk-sized; sexes similar; white head and body; gray back; pink legs; dark wing tips; yellow eyes; red spot on lower mandible (seen only at close range). *Immature:* variable; brown overall.
Size: 24–26 in.

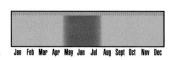

| Jan | Feb | Mar | Apr | May | Jun | Jul | Aug | Sept | Oct | Nov | Dec |

Common Tern
Sterna hirundo

The Common Tern generally goes unnoticed until a splash draws attention to its headfirst dives into water. Once it has firmly seized a small fish in its black-tipped bill, the tern bounces back into the air and continues its leisurely flight. Common Terns are easily observed in May, working the shores of Lake Erie Metropark during migration. Although some terns remain to nest, most choose to continue north for breeding opportunities.

Although terns and gulls share many of the same physical characteristics, there are features that clearly separate the two groups. Terns seldom rest on the water, and they rarely soar in flight. They also have very short necks, pointed wings and long, forked tails, and they tend to look toward the ground during flight. Both gulls and terns tend to nest in similar regions, but this may be more convenient for the gulls because they routinely prey on the smaller terns.

Similar Species: Caspian Tern (p. 61) has a large, red bill and is gull-sized. Forster's Tern has a grayer tail and frosted wing tips.

breeding

Quick I.D.: larger than a pigeon; sexes similar; black cap; orange bill tipped with black; gray back and wings; pointed wings; white throat and belly. *In flight:* forked tail; often hovers.
Size: 14–16 in.

Jan Feb Mar Apr May Jun Jul Aug Sept Oct Nov Dec

Caspian Tern
Sterna caspia

breeding

The Caspian Tern seems to bridge the gulf between gulls and terns. It appears equally at ease roosting among similarly sized gulls or flying stiffly and lazily while pointing its coral red bill toward the water. This species never reaches the abundance of many other gulls and terns in our area, but its formidable size results in a second look each spring from birders who have grown accustomed to the sights of the more common species.

Perhaps no other bird possesses such an odd North American breeding distribution as the Caspian Tern. Isolated colonies of Caspian Terns breed in pockets around the Great Lakes, in Utah, in Wyoming, in British Columbia, in the Northwest Territories, in Newfoundland and along the Pacific Coast of the United States.

Similar Species: Common Tern (p. 60) and Forster's Tern are both much smaller and lack the heavy, red bill. Ring-billed Gull (p. 58) lacks the red bill and the black cap. Bonaparte's Gull (p. 57) has a black hood and bill.

Quick I.D.: gull-sized; sexes similar; black cap; heavy, blood-red bill; light gray wing covers; white underparts; black legs.
In flight: shallowly forked tail; long, pointed wings; head often points downward.
Size: 19–22¹/₂ in.

Jan Feb Mar Apr May Jun Jul Aug Sept Oct Nov Dec

Rock Dove
Columba livia

The Rock Dove (Pigeon) is very dependent on humans for food and shelter. This Eurasian native lives in old buildings, on ledges and on bridges, and it feeds primarily on waste grain and human handouts. It was first brought to North America in 1606 as a food source. Rock Doves have had the last laugh, though, because they quickly dispersed from the East Coast to colonize the entire continent.

Rock Doves may appear strained when they walk—their heads move back and forth with every step—but few birds are as agile in flight or as abundant in urban and industrial areas. Although no other bird varies as much in coloration, all Rock Doves, whether white, red, blue or mixed-pigment, will clap their wings above and below their bodies upon take-off.

Similar Species: Mourning Dove (p. 63) is the same length as the Rock Dove, but it is slender and has a long, tapering tail and olive-brown plumage.

Quick I.D.: mid-sized pigeon; sexes similar; variable color (iridescent blue-gray, black, red or white); white rump (usually); orange feet; fleshy base to bill.

Size: 13–14 in.

Jan Feb Mar Apr May Jun Jul Aug Sept Oct Nov Dec

Mourning Dove
Zenaida macroura

As a Mourning Dove bursts into flight, its wings 'clap' above and below its body for the first few wing beats. The Mourning Dove is a swift, direct flier, and its wings can be heard whistling through the air. When not in flight, the peaceful *coooah-coooo-cooooo-coooo!* call of the Mourning Dove can be heard filtering through open woodlands. These year-round residents roost inconspicuously in trees, but their soft cooing often betrays their presence.

The Mourning Dove feeds primarily on the ground, picking up grain and grit in open areas. It builds a flat, loose stick nest that rests flimsily on branches and trunks. Mourning Doves are attentive parents, and, like other members of the pigeon family, they feed 'milk' to their young. It isn't true milk—since birds lack mammary glands—but a fluid produced by glands in the bird's crop. The chicks insert their bills down the adult's throat to eat the thick liquid.

Similar Species: Rock Dove (p. 62) has a white rump, is stockier and has a shorter tail.

Quick I.D: jay-sized; sexes similar; gray-brown plumage; long, white-trimmed, tapering tail; sleek body; dark, shiny patch below ear; orange feet; dark bill; buff-colored underparts.
Size: 11–13 in.

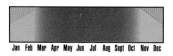

Jan Feb Mar Apr May Jun Jul Aug Sept Oct Nov Dec

Eastern Screech-Owl
Otus asio

Despite its small size, the Eastern Screech-Owl is a versatile hunter. It has a varied diet that ranges from insects, earthworms and fish to birds larger than itself. Silent and reclusive by day, screech-owls hunt at night. Strolling along the roadsides of Bald Mountain State Recreation Area during an early spring evening, a person with a keen ear will hear the distinctive, whistled whinny voice of the Eastern Screech-Owl.

Some owls' senses are refined for darkness and their bodies for silence. Their large, forward-facing eyes have many times more light-gathering sensors than do ours, and the wings of nocturnal owls are edged with frayed feathers for silent flight. Their ears, which occupy a large part of the sides of their heads, are asymmetrical (one is higher than the other), which enables these birds to pinpoint sounds more easily. Given these adaptations, it is no surprise that owls have successfully invaded nearly all of the world's major ecosystems.

Similar Species: Northern Saw-whet Owl has a dark facial disc and no ear tufts.

Quick I.D.: robin-sized; sexes similar; short, widely spaced ear tufts; heavy vertical streaking and bars on chest; yellow eyes; dark bill; two color phases (gray, which is more common, and red.)
Size: 8–9 in. (female slightly larger).

Jan Feb Mar Apr May Jun Jul Aug Sept Oct Nov Dec

Great Horned Owl
Bubo virginianus

The Great Horned Owl is the most widely distributed owl in North America, and it is among the most formidable of predators. It uses specialized hearing, powerful talons and human-sized eyes during nocturnal hunts for mice, rabbits, quails, amphibians and occasionally fish. It has a poorly developed sense of smell, which is why it can (and frequently does) prey on skunks—worn-out and discarded Great Horned Owl feathers are often identifiable by a simple sniff.

The deep, resonant hooting of the Great Horned Owl is easily imitated, often leading to interesting exchanges between bird and birder. The call's deep tone is not as distinctive as its pace, which closely follows the rhythm of *eat my food, I'll-eat yooou!*

Similar Species: Eastern Screech-Owl (p. 64) is much smaller and has vertical breast streaking. Long-eared Owl has a slimmer body and vertical streaks on its chest, and its ear tufts are very close together.

Quick I.D.: hawk-sized; sexes similar; large, widely spaced ear tufts; fine, horizontal chest bars; dark brown plumage; white throat.
Size: 18–25 in.

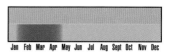

Jan Feb Mar Apr May Jun Jul Aug Sept Oct Nov Dec

Common Nighthawk
Chordeiles minor

The Common Nighthawk, which is unrelated to true hawks, has two distinct personalities: mild-mannered by day, it rests on the ground or on a horizontal tree branch, its color and shape blending perfectly into the texture of the bark; at dusk, the Common Nighthawk takes on a new form as a dazzling and erratic flyer, catching insects in flight. It is most conspicuous in its late August migrations.

To many people, the sounds of the nighthawk are the sounds of summer evenings, and the recent declines in their numbers have left many naturalists longing for the previously common calls. The fascinating courtship of Common Nighthawks occurs over forest openings, beaches and urban areas. The nighthawks repeatedly call out with a loud, nasal *peeent!* as they circle high overhead; then they dive suddenly toward the ground and create a hollow *vroom* by thrusting their wings forward at the last possible moment, pulling out of the dive.

Similar Species: Whip-poor-will has a rounded tail and wings.

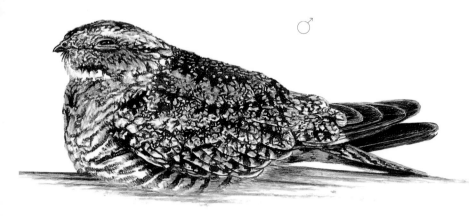

♂

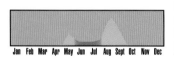

Jan Feb Mar Apr May Jun Jul Aug Sept Oct Nov Dec

Quick I.D.: robin-sized; sexes similar; cryptic light to dark brown; pale throat. *In flight:* long, pointed wings; white wrist bands; shallowly forked tail; flight is erratic.
Size: 9–10 in.

Belted Kingfisher
Ceryle alcyon

♀

♂

The Belted Kingfisher is found near quiet waters, never far from shore. As the name suggests, kingfishers primarily prey on fish, which they catch with precise, headfirst dives. A dead branch extending over water will often serve as a perch from which they can survey the fish below.

The Belted Kingfisher builds its nest near the end of a long tunnel excavated a few feet into a sandy or dirt bank. A rattling call—similar to a teacup shaking on a saucer—blue-gray coloration and a large crest are the distinctive features of the Belted Kingfisher. In most birds, the males are more colorful, but female kingfishers are distinguished from males by the presence of a second, rust-colored band across the belly.

Although there are many species of kingfishers in the world, the Belted Kingfisher is the only member of its family across most of the United States. Where open water is found in the Detroit area, Belted Kingfishers can be encountered crashing into calm waters in search of fish.

Similar Species: None.

Quick I.D.: pigeon-sized; blue-gray back, wings and head; shaggy crest; heavy bill; blue chest band. *Female:* rust-colored belt.
Size: 12–14 in.

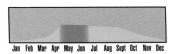

Jan Feb Mar Apr May Jun Jul Aug Sept Oct Nov Dec

KINGFISHERS 67

Red-headed Woodpecker
Melanerpes erythrocephalus

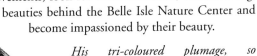

When Alexander Wilson landed in North America, with little money and few skills, he did not know what he'd do with his life. Like a revelation, a Red-headed Woodpecker was one of the first birds to greet the Scotsman. Never had Wilson seen such beauty, and the bird inspired the future 'father of American ornithology' to devote his life to birds. With no formal ornithological background, he went on to discover and describe dozens of North American species.

Although the Red-headed Woodpecker's plumage may not drive everyone to great scientific achievements, look for these wondrous, but declining, beauties behind the Belle Isle Nature Center and become impassioned by their beauty.

> *His tri-coloured plumage, so striking.... A gay and frolicsome disposition, diving and vociferating around the high dead limbs of some large tree, amusing the passenger with their gambols.*
>
> *—Alexander Wilson*

Similar Species: Red-bellied Woodpecker (p. 69) has gray cheeks and black and white 'zebra' stripes on its back.

Quick I.D.: robin-sized; sexes similar; stunning red head and throat; black back and tail; white rump, inner wing patches and belly. *Immature:* brownish head; bars on white wing patch; dirty white underparts. **Size:** 8–9 in.

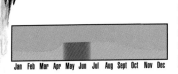

Jan Feb Mar Apr May Jun Jul Aug Sept Oct Nov Dec

Red-bellied Woodpecker
Melanerpes carolinus

An unexpected vocal *churr*, like a bark, emanating from deciduous woodlands throughout our area is often the first clue that the oddly named Red-bellied Woodpecker is about. A fairly common resident in our area, this woodpecker acquired a name that reflects a very subtle field mark. Because the 'Red-Headed' moniker belongs to a more deserving woodpecker, perhaps a better name would have been the 'Zebra-backed Woodpecker.'

This woodpecker has recently enjoyed a slight increase in numbers in our area, mostly because the regeneration of Midwestern forests has encouraged dispersal of these birds from the south. Birdfeeders have also helped Red-bellied Woodpeckers survive our harsh winters. Many Detroit birdwatchers fondly remember the chilly winter day when this striking bird first visited their sunflower seed feeder. Even if the seed source is completely reliable, Red-bellied Woodpeckers take no chances; they hoard the food, filling tree cavities, gaps in shingles, and other small spaces with seeds.

Similar Species: Red-headed Woodpecker (p. 68) has a solid red head and a solid black upper back. Northern Flicker (p. 72) has black-spotted underparts and yellow wing and tail linings and lacks the black-and-white barring on the back.

Quick I.D.: robin-sized; black-and-white barring on back; red crown and nape; plain gray face and underparts; very faint red belly; white rump. *Male:* red forehead. *Female:* gray forehead.
Size: 9 in.

Jan Feb Mar Apr May Jun Jul Aug Sept Oct Nov Dec

Downy Woodpecker
Picoides pubescens

Soft taps carry through a quiet forest, sounding out the activities of a Downy Woodpecker. It methodically searches for hidden invertebrates by chipping off dead bark and probing into crevices. This woodpecker's small bill is amazingly effective at removing tiny slabs of bark, which rain down to the forest floor. The Downy Woodpecker is a systematic forager, and because of its small bill, it can find food where larger-billed woodpeckers cannot reach. Only when all the nooks of a tree have been probed will the Downy look about and give a chipper note before moving on to explore neighboring trees.

This black-and-white bird is the smallest North American woodpecker, and it is common in almost any woodlot. It's easily attracted to backyard feeders by suet. The male is readily distinguished from the female by a small patch of red feathers on the back of his head.

Similar Species: Hairy Woodpecker (p. 71) is larger and has a longer bill and clean white outer tail feathers.

Quick I.D.: large sparrow–sized; black-and-white wings and back; unmarked, white underparts; short, stubby bill; white outer tail feathers are spotted black.
Male: red patch on back of head.
Female: no red patch.
Size: 6–7 in.

Jan Feb Mar Apr May Jun Jul Aug Sept Oct Nov Dec

Hairy Woodpecker
Picoides villosus

The Hairy Woodpecker looks like an overgrown Downy Woodpecker, and it shares the habitat of its smaller cousin. Although it is not as common nor as easily approached as a Downy, the Hairy's loud calls and hammering enliven an empty winter forest. Its long, dark bill hammers rotting wood apart, exposing the soft-bodied, larval invertebrates inside.

Many woodpeckers depend on dead and dying trees for nest sites and stable food sources. The perception that dead wood and old trees are waste is a view not shared by many species of woodpecker. By hammering apart old logs and feeding on invertebrates, woodpeckers contribute to the renewal process inherent in natural systems.

Although Hairy Woodpeckers can be seen every day of the year in the Detroit area, they are more frequently seen in winter, when the leaves are off the trees and the birds are busy feeding. This mid-sized woodpecker can be often encountered foraging diligently in many city parks and backyards.

Similar Species: Downy Woodpecker (p. 70) is smaller and has a shorter bill. Red-headed Woodpecker (p. 68) has an all-red head.

Quick I.D.: smaller than a robin; black-and-white back and wings; white underparts; bill as long as head is wide; no black spots on white outer tail feathers.
Male: red patch on back of head.
Female: no red patch.
Size: 8–9 in.

Jan Feb Mar Apr May Jun Jul Aug Sept Oct Nov Dec

Northern Flicker

Colaptes auratus

Walkers strolling through any of our larger parks may be surprised by a woodpecker flushing from the ground before them. As the Northern Flicker beats a hasty retreat, it reveals an unmistakable white rump and yellow wing linings. It is the least arboreal of our woodpeckers, and it spends more time feeding on the ground than other woodpeckers. Often, it is only when the Northern Flicker is around its nest cavity in a tree that it truly behaves like other woodpeckers: clinging, rattling and drumming.

The Northern Flicker can be seen all year. It occasionally visits backyard feeders, but it is certainly less abundant through our winters. The Northern Flicker—and other birds—squash ants and then preen themselves with the remains. Ants contain concentrations of formic acid, which is believed to kill small parasites living on the flicker's skin and in its feathers.

Similar Species: Red-bellied Woodpecker (p. 69) has a red crown and black and white bars on its back.

Jan Feb Mar Apr May Jun Jul Aug Sept Oct Nov Dec

Quick I.D.: jay-sized; brown-barred back; spotted underparts; black bib; white rump; long bill; yellow wing and tail linings; gray crown; red nape. *Male:* black mustache. *Female:* no mustache.
Size: 11–14 in.

Ruby-throated Hummingbird
Archilochus colubris

You are fortunate if you are one the few people to get a prolonged look at a Ruby-throated Hummingbird, the only eastern hummingbird. Most meetings are over before they begin—a loud hum draws your attention to a small object flitting about, but it quickly disappears through the trees. It's often only after the bird has disappeared that its identity becomes apparent.

Fortunately, Ruby-throated Hummingbirds are easily attracted to feeders of sweetened water (one part white sugar to four parts water). The male's iridescent ruby throat and emerald back play with the sunlight in ever-switching colors. The Ruby-throated Hummingbird's gentle appearance is misleading: these fiercely aggressive hummingbirds will chase intruders away in spirited defense of a food source or prospective mates.

Similar Species: None.

Quick I.D.: our smallest bird; iridescent green back; long, thin, dark bill.
Male: iridescent ruby throat.
Size: 4 in.

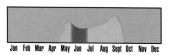

Jan Feb Mar Apr May Jun Jul Aug Sept Oct Nov Dec

Eastern Wood-Pewee
Contopus virens

The plaintive, sad whistle—*pee-wee* or *pee-a-wee*—of the Eastern Wood-Pewee echoes though most woodlands in our area. These mouse-colored summer visitors are difficult to see until they loop out after a passing insect. A classic flycatcher, the Eastern Wood-Pewee faithfully returns to its preferred perch, at the mid-level in the forest, following each short foraging flight.

The nest of the Eastern Wood-Pewee resembles nothing more than a knot on a small limb. It is extremely well camouflaged by both shape and color—the outer walls are wall-papered with lichens—and it looks too small for the bird to fit in it. As an additional precaution, these small flycatchers vigorously defend their nest site against all intruders who dare approach.

Similar Species: Least Flycatcher (p. 75) has an eye ring and sings a steady *che bek* song. Acadian Flycatcher has an eye ring and sings an emphatic *peet-sah!*

Quick I.D.: sparrow-sized; sexes similar; olive-gray body; dark tail and wings; two faint wing bars; no eye ring; dark upper mandible; pale orange lower mandible.
Size: 6–6½ in.

Jan Feb Mar Apr May Jun Jul Aug Sept Oct Nov Dec

Least Flycatcher

Empidonax minimus

Southern spring winds carry the first Least Flycatchers into Michigan's forests in early May. The day of their arrival is often easily recognized, because these small birds punctuate their presence with their simple and steady *che-bek* song. From naked perches, inches from the trunks of trees, Least Flycatchers sing and survey their chosen territories.

Although it nests sparsely in our area, such as at Metro Beach Metropark, the Least Flycatcher is noticeable because it is one of the boldest and most pugnacious songbirds in the deciduous forests in Michigan. It is noisy and aggressive, driving away all avian intruders. Male Least Flycatchers reach their peak of aggression during the courtship season, when they fight furiously with rival males. Because their extroverted behaviors outweigh their somber plumage, even the handful of breeders in our parks can be encountered with a little effort most summers.

Similar Species: Eastern Wood-Pewee (p. 74) lacks the eye ring and sings *pee-a-wee*. Willow Flycatcher has a faint eye ring. Acadian Flycatcher sings *peet-sah!*

Quick I.D.: sparrow-sized; sexes similar; olive brown upperparts; two white wing bars; light-colored eye ring; long, narrow tail; dark bill; light throat; dark tail.
Size: 5 in.

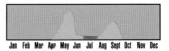

Jan Feb Mar Apr May Jun Jul Aug Sept Oct Nov Dec

Eastern Phoebe
Sayornis phoebe

Although many birds pump their tails while perched, no bird can match the zest and frequency of the Eastern Phoebe's tail wag. This early spring migrant might lack a distinctive plumage, but its identity is never questioned when the quick and jerky tail rises and falls. Keeping in perfect synchrony with its rhythmic rump, the Eastern Phoebe's voice joins in accompaniment. As its name suggests, this small flycatcher bolts out a cheery *fee-bee* from an exposed spring perch.

The Eastern Phoebe is one of the first songbirds to return in spring. It frequently builds its nest on buildings, and it has shown an ability to adapt to altered environments. A nest site might be used repeatedly over the years, or a new site might be chosen annually. Whatever the case, the Eastern Phoebe's nest is always protected from the rain by a roof.

Similar Species: *Empidonax* flycatchers have wing bars. Eastern Wood-Pewee (p. 74) is smaller and has a different voice.

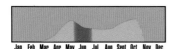

Jan Feb Mar Apr May Jun Jul Aug Sept Oct Nov Dec

Quick I.D.: larger than a sparrow; sexes similar; brownish-gray back; no wing bars or eye ring; dark tail, wings and head. *Breeding:* white belly. *Non-breeding:* yellowish belly.
Size: 6 1/2–7 in.

Great Crested Flycatcher
Myiarchus crinitus

The Great Crested Flycatcher's name is somewhat misleading. A glimpse of this bird at Fairlane Woods or in any Oakland County woodland would leave the observer with the impression that it is simply a Great Flycatcher. Closer inspection of the bird might reveal a small crest, but certainly nothing to rival a Blue Jay or Northern Cardinal.

The Great Crested Flycatcher has an unusual taste in decor for its nest cavity: it occasionally lays a shed snakeskin as a door mat. This uncommon, but noteworthy, practice can identify the nest of this flycatcher, the only member of its family in Detroit to nest in a cavity. The purpose of the snakeskin is not known, and these versatile birds have occasionally substituted plastic wrap for reptilian skin.

Similar Species: Eastern Wood-Pewee (p. 74), Eastern Phoebe (p. 76) and other flycatchers are smaller and lack the lemon yellow belly and the chestnut tail lining.

Quick I.D.: smaller than a robin; sexes similar; yellow belly; gray throat and head; dark back and wings; chestnut tail lining; rufous wing linings; erect crest.
Size: 7–8 in.

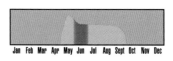

Jan Feb Mar Apr May Jun Jul Aug Sept Oct Nov Dec

Eastern Kingbird
Tyrannus tyrannus

When one thinks of a tyrant, images of a large carnivorous dinosaur or a menacing ruler are much more likely to come to mind than the image of a little bird. The Eastern Kingbird may not initially seem to be as imposing as other known tyrants, but this flycatcher certainly lives up to its scientific name, *Tyrannus tyrannus*. The Eastern Kingbird is pugnacious—it will fearlessly attack crows, hawks, other large birds and even humans that pass through its territory. The intruders are often vigorously pursued, pecked and plucked for some distance, until the kingbird is satisfied that there is no further threat.

The courtship flight of the Eastern Kingbird, which can be seen in fields and shrubby areas, is characterized by short, quivering wing beats—a touching display even for this little tyrant.

Similar Species: All other flycatchers and Tree Swallow (p. 81) lack the white, terminal tail band and are not black and white.

Quick I.D.: smaller than a robin; sexes similar; black head, back, wings and tail; white underparts; white terminal tail band; orange-red crown (rarely seen). **Size:** 9 in.

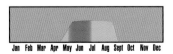

Jan Feb Mar Apr May Jun Jul Aug Sept Oct Nov Dec

Chimney Swift
Chaetura pelagica

The Chimney Swift is one of the frequent fliers of the bird world; only raising a family keeps this bird off its wings. It feeds, drinks, bathes and even mates in flight. During its four- to five-year average lifespan, these sailors of the air can travel more than one million miles. These high-flying aeronauts often forage for flying insects at great heights, and during the height of day they are visible only as sky specks. As the sun sinks to the horizon, however, flocks of Chimney Swifts can be seen spiraling into their evening roosts.

Swifts are shaped much like swallows—long, tapering wings, a small bill, a wide gape and a long, sleek body—but they share no close relationship. The wing beats of swifts looks uncomfortable, but it doesn't hamper the graceful flight of these aerial masters, who cast a distinct boomerang silhouette when they glide. Swifts, when not in flight, use their small but strong claws to cling precariously to vertical surfaces. Because many old, hollow hardwood trees have been removed since colonization, Chimney Swifts have adopted human structures, such as chimneys, as common nesting sites.

Similar Species: All swallows have smooth, direct flight and broader wings.

Quick I.D.: smaller than a sparrow; sexes similar; brown overall; slim. *In flight:* rapid wing beats and erratic, boomerang flight profile.
Size: 5¹/₂ in.

Jan Feb Mar Apr May Jun Jul Aug Sept Oct Nov Dec

Purple Martin
Progne subis

Late summer is a very busy time around a Purple Martin complex. Adults spiral around the large, communal next box, coming and going in foraging forays. The year's young perch at the openings of their apartment cavities, impatiently waiting for their parents to return with a mouthful of flying insects. A patient observer will notice how orderly the apparent confusion is to the martin, and how efficiently the crowded complex is negotiated.

These fascinating experiences are rewards to residents who erect Purple Martin complexes, which should be high on a pole in the middle of a large, open area. The complex should be cleaned and plugged up once the birds have left, until they return in spring. House Sparrows and starlings will overthrow the preferred tenant if given a chance.

Similar Species: Barn Swallow (p. 82) has a deeply forked tail. Tree Swallow (p. 81) has a white belly. European Starling (p. 118) has a long bill and a short tail.

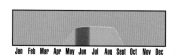

Jan Feb Mar Apr May Jun Jul Aug Sept Oct Nov Dec

Quick I.D.: smaller than a robin; deep, glossy blue; pointed wings; forked tail; small bill. *Female* and *Immature:* gray underparts; duller backs.
Size: 7–8 in.

Tree Swallow
Tachycineta bicolor

Depending on food availability, Tree Swallows might forage for great distances, darting above open fields and wetlands as they catch flying insects in their bills. These bicolored birds occasionally sweep down to the water surface for a quick drink and bath. In bad weather, Tree Swallows might fly up to five miles to distant marshes or lakes to find flying insects.

The Tree Swallow is among the first migrants to arrive in the Detroit area, often beating the onset of spring weather. It returns to freshwater marshes by late March to begin its reproductive cycle in late April. It nests in abandoned woodpecker cavities as well as in nest boxes. The cavity is lined with weeds, grasses and long feathers. When the parents leave the eggs for long periods of time, the swallows cover them with the feathers. The females lay and incubate four to six eggs for up to 16 days. Once the birds hatch, the young leave the cavity within three weeks to begin their aerial lives.

Similar Species: Chimney Swift (p. 79) has slimmer wings and a darker belly. Northern Rough-winged Swallow and Bank Swallow lack the blue-green upperparts.

Quick I.D.: sparrow-sized; sexes similar; iridescent blue-green plumage; white underparts; dark rump; small bill; small feet. *In flight:* long, pointed wings; shallowly forked tail.
Size: 5–6 in.

Barn Swallow
Hirundo rustica

The graceful flight of this bird is a common summer sight. It often forages at low altitudes, so its deeply forked tail is easily observed. The Barn Swallow is actually the only swallow in Detroit to have a 'swallow-tail.' The name 'swallow' originated in Europe (it comes from the Old Norse *svala*), where the Barn Swallow is also common, and where it is simply called the Swallow. (The verb 'to swallow' comes from a different root: the Old Norse *svelgr*, 'a whirlpool.')

The Barn Swallow builds its cup-shaped mud nest in the eaves of barns and picnic shelters, or in any other structure that provides protection from the rain. Because the Barn Swallow is often closely associated with human structures, it is not uncommon for a nervous parent bird to dive repeatedly at human 'intruders,' encouraging them to retreat.

Similar Species: Purple Martin (p. 80) has a shorter tail and lacks the russet throat and forehead.

Quick I.D.: larger than a sparrow; sexes similar, but female is a bit duller; deeply forked tail; glossy blue back, wings and tail; buffy underparts; russet throat and forehead.
Size: 6–8 in.

Jan Feb Mar Apr May Jun Jul Aug Sept Oct Nov Dec

Blue Jay
Cyanocitta cristata

The Detroit area, with its broken forests and plentiful birdfeeders, must look a lot like Blue Jay heaven. One of the region's most identifiable birds—with its loud *jay-jay-jay* call, its blue-and-white plumage and its large crest—the Blue Jay is familiar to anyone with sunflower seeds or peanuts at their birdfeeder. Blue Jays are intelligent, aggressive and adaptable birds that don't hesitate to drive smaller birds, squirrels or even cats away when they feel threatened.

The Blue Jay represents all the admirable virtues and aggressive qualities of the corvid family. While it is beautiful, resourceful and vocally diverse, the Blue Jay can be one of the most annoying and mischievous birds, and no predator is too formidable for this bird to harass. With noisy calls, Blue Jays wake up neighborhoods and forests where they are the self-appointed guardians. This colorful bird's extroverted character and boldness outweigh its occasional, briefly annoying behavior.

Similar Species: None.

Quick I.D.: larger than a robin; sexes similar; blue crest, back wings and tail; black necklace; white wing bars; light belly.
Size: 11–12 in.

Jan Feb Mar Apr May Jun Jul Aug Sept Oct Nov Dec

American Crow
Corvus brachyrhynchos

The American Crow calls with the classic, long, descending *caaaw*. Throughout the year, this common bird announces the start of the day to Detroit-area residents. In late summer and fall, when their reproductive duties are completed, crows group together to roost in flocks, known as a 'murders.' The crow population has increased in our area in recent years, and large flocks can be seen almost anywhere in the Detroit area.

This large, black bird's intelligence has led it into many confrontations with humans, from which it often emerges the victor. Scientific studies have shown that crows are capable of solving simple problems, which comes as no surprise to anyone who has watched a crow snip open garbage bags with scissor-like precision.

Similar Species: None.

Jan Feb Mar Apr May Jun Jul Aug Sept Oct Nov Dec

Quick I.D.: small gull–sized; sexes similar; black; fan-shaped tail; slim overall.
Size: 18–20 in.

Black-capped Chickadee
Poecile atricapillus

The Black-capped Chickadee is one of the most pleasant birds in urban and forested areas, often seeming to greet walkers along trails. It is a common sight in Detroit and can be found in every park and in most landscaped backyards. Throughout most of the year, chickadees move about in loose flocks, investigating nooks and crannies for food and uttering their delicate *chick-a-dee-dee-dee* calls.

During spring, Black-capped Chickadees seem strangely absent from city parks and wooded ravines: while nesting, they remain inconspicuous. Once the first fall chill arrives, the woods are once again vibrant with their busy activities.

Similar Species: Tufted Titmouse (p. 86) lacks the black cap and bib. White-breasted Nuthatch (p. 87) lacks the black chin and has a short tail and long bill. Blackpoll Warbler (p. 106) is a migrant with orange legs and streaked underparts.

Quick I.D.: smaller than a sparrow; sexes similar; black cap and bib; white cheek; grayish back, wings and tail; light underparts.
Size: 5–6 in.

Jan Feb Mar Apr May Jun Jul Aug Sept Oct Nov Dec

Tufted Titmouse
Baeolophus bicolor

An inquisitive Tufted Titmouse perches a short flight away from a well-stocked backyard feeder. On this breaking spring day, its persistent whistle ebbs *peter peter peter* throughout the neighborhood. Throughout much of the year, the Tufted Titmouse is a familiar neighbor in many Detroit-area communities, gracing backyards with its trusting inquisitions.

Tufted Titmice can be found nesting in most woodlands. They choose abandoned cavities, previously occupied and excavated by small woodpeckers, in which to build their nest. In these cozy homes they line their nests with hair boldly plucked from dogs, wild animals or even humans. You can remove the hair accumulated in your hairbrush and set it out in your yard as a delightful way to draw the birds in; they will incorporate a small part of you in the wildness of your neighborhood.

Similar Species: None.

Quick I.D.: sparrow-sized; sexes similar; small crest; dark gray upperparts; light gray underparts; reddish flanks; small black forehead.
Size: 5–6 in.

Jan Feb Mar Apr May Jun Jul Aug Sept Oct Nov Dec

White-breasted Nuthatch
Sitta carolinensis

The White-breasted Nuthatch is a curious bird. To the novice bird-watcher, seeing a nuthatch call repeatedly while clinging to the underside of a branch is an odd sight. To nuthatches, however, this gravity-defying act is as natural as flight is to other birds. Nuthatches frequently pause in mid-descent, arching their head out at right angles to the trunk and giving their distinctive and often repeated nasal *anh-anh-anh-anh* call. They make their seemingly dangerous headfirst hops look routine.

White-breasted Nuthatches frequently visit backyard feeders. They seem less at home on the level platform feeders, where they cast aside their tree-trunk talent for an easy meal of sunflower seeds.

Similar Species: Red-breasted Nuthatch has a red breast and a black eye line. Black-capped Chickadee (p. 85) has a black bib and a longer tail.

♂

Quick I.D.: sparrow-sized. *Male:* black cap; white cheeks and breast; steel-blue back, wings and tail; straight bill; short tail; russet undertail coverts. *Female:* similar, but with a grayish cap.
Size: 6 in.

Jan Feb Mar Apr May Jun Jul Aug Sept Oct Nov Dec

House Wren
Troglodytes aedon

This common bird of suburbs, city parks and woodlands sings as though its lungs were bottomless. The sweet, warbling song of the House Wren is distinguished by its melodious tone and its uninterrupted endurance. Although the House Wren is far smaller than a sparrow, it offers an unending song in one breath.

Like all wrens, the House Wren frequently carries its short tail cocked straight up. This bird is often observed in woodlands, city parks and backyards, skulking beneath the dense understorey, from May to September. As spring arrives, the House Wren treats Detroit neighborhoods to a few weeks of wonderful warbles before it channels its energy to the task of reproduction.

Similar Species: Winter Wren's tail is shorter than its legs. Carolina Wren is larger and has a white eyebrow.

Quick I.D.: smaller than a sparrow; sexes similar; brown; tail often cocked up; bill slightly downcurved; tail as long as legs.
Size: 5 in.

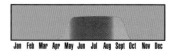

Jan Feb Mar Apr May Jun Jul Aug Sept Oct Nov Dec

Golden-crowned Kinglet
Regulus satrapa

♀

♂

The high-pitched, tinkling voice of the Golden-crowned Kinglet is as familiar as the sweet smell of pine and fir in coniferous forests. Although this bird is not immediately obvious to the uninformed passerby, a birdwatcher with a keen ear, patience and the willingness to draw down this smallest of North American songbirds with squeaks and pishes will encounter kinglets on many outdoor trips. During April and then again in October and November, Detroit's parks and older communities come alive with the sound of the Golden-crowned Kinglet's faint, high-pitched *tsee-tsee-tsee-tsee.*

As these tiny birds descend in loose flocks around a curious onlooker, their indistinct plumage and voice offer little excitement. It is when the flock circles nearby, using the branches as swings and trapezes, flashing their regal crowns, that the magic of the kinglet emerges.

Similar Species: Ruby-crowned Kinglet (p. 90) lacks the black outline to the crown.

Quick I.D.: smaller than a sparrow; plump; dark olive; white wing bars; dark tail and wings; white eyebrow. *Male:* fiery orange crown bordered by black. *Female:* lemon yellow crown bordered by black.
Size: 4 in.

Jan Feb Mar Apr May Jun Jul Aug Sept Oct Nov Dec

Ruby-crowned Kinglet
Regulus calendula

These kinglets are common migrants to Detroit parks and woodlands. They visit in September and October and again in April and May, flitting continuously through our shrubs. Kinglets always appear nervous: their tails and wings flick continually as they hop from branch to branch in search of grubs and insect eggs.

The Ruby-crowned Kinglet is similar to the Golden-crowned Kinglet in size, habits and coloration, except that it has a hidden ruby crown. 'Rubies' are heard more often then they are seen, especially as spring approaches. Their distinctive song starts like a motor chugging to life, and then the kinglets fire off a series of loud, rising *chewy-chewy-chewy-chewys*. These final, excitable phrases are often the only recognizable part of the song.

Similar Species: Golden-crowned Kinglet (p. 89) has a black outline to the crown.

Quick I.D.: smaller than a sparrow; plump; dark olive; white wing bars; dark tail and wings; eye ring. *Male:* red crown (infrequently seen). *Female:* no red crown.
Size: 4 in.

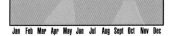

Jan Feb Mar Apr May Jun Jul Aug Sept Oct Nov Dec

Eastern Bluebird
Sialia sialis

Dressed with the colors of the cool sky on his back and the warm setting sun on his breast, the male Eastern Bluebird looks like a piece of pure sky come to life. To fully appreciate this specialty, try to spot a male as he sets up his territory on a crisp, early spring morning in open country, such as in Oakwoods Metropark, Stony Creek Metropark and many other rural settings in the Detroit area.

The Eastern Bluebird lost many of its nesting sites in natural cavities to House Sparrows and European Starlings and to the removal of dead trees from southeastern Michigan. Concerned residents rallied for this bird, however, and put up thousands of nesting boxes to compensate for the losses. The Eastern Bluebird population has slowly increased as a result, and the vigilant residents have been rewarded with the sight of the bird's beautiful plumage in the Midwest's landscape.

Similar Species: Male Indigo Bunting (p. 141) lacks the red breast and has a conical bill.

♂

Quick I.D.: smaller than a robin. *Male:* blue back; red throat and breast; white undertail coverts; thin bill. *Female:* more washed out and less intense blue.
Size: 6–7 in.

Jan Feb Mar Apr May Jun Jul Aug Sept Oct Nov Dec

Veery
Catharus fuscescens

Like a tumbling waterfall, the Veery's voice descends with a liquid ripple. This bird, like all other thrushes, is a master of melodies, and it offers its unequaled songs to dusky forests. It is one of the last singers in the evening. Listen for a audio treat at Bald Mountain State Recreation Area or Fairlane Woods during the first weeks of June.

The Veery is perhaps the most terrestrial of Detroit's thrushes, and it frequently nests on the ground. In characteristic thrush style, the Veery searches for grubs and caterpillars by shuffling through loose leaf litter. When an invertebrate delicacy is found, it is swallowed quickly, and the ever-vigilant Veery cautiously looks about before renewing the hunt.

Similar Species: Wood Thrush (p. 94), Hermit Thrush (p. 93) and Swainson's Thrush are more boldly patterned on the breast and each has a characteristic song.

Jan Feb Mar Apr May Jun Jul Aug Sept Oct Nov Dec

Quick I.D.: smaller than a robin; sexes similar; reddish-brown head, back, rump and tail; faint spotting on throat; no conspicuous eye ring.
Size: 7–8 in.

Hermit Thrush
Catharus guttatus

Beauty in forest birds is often gauged by sound and not appearance. Given this criterion, the Hermit Thrush is certainly one of the most beautiful birds to pass through Detroit-area woodlands. A migrant to boreal forests, Hermit Thrushes are heard but rarely seen during their all too brief month passage, revealing themselves mainly when flocking together during the southern migration.

The upward spiral in the song of the Hermit Thrush lifts the soul with each note, and leaves a fortunate listener breathless at its conclusion. The inspiring song is heard on early spring mornings, but it is most appreciated at dusk, when the Hermit Thrush offers an emotional melody to the darkening forest.

Similar Species: Swainson's Thrush lacks the reddish rump and tail and has buffy-olive cheeks. Fox Sparrow (p. 124) has a short conical bill.

Quick I.D.: smaller than a robin; sexes similar; reddish-brown rump and tail; olive-brown head and back; light eye ring; olive-brown spots on upper chest; light underparts.
Size: 7–8 in.

Jan Feb Mar Apr May Jun Jul Aug Sept Oct Nov Dec

Wood Thrush
Hylocichla mustelina

The Wood Thrushes musical warble—*Will you live with me? Way up high in a tree, I'll come right down and ... seeee!*—has sadly faded from many Michigan woodlands. The Wood Thrush was once the voice of our hardwood forests, but it has declined because of forest fragmentation. As the woodlands disappear, this songster follows their path toward silence. Broken forests invite common open-area predators and parasites, such as the skunk, fox, crow, jay and cowbird, which traditionally had no access to Wood Thrush nests insulated deep within the protected confines of vast hardwoods.

Like the hope and faith that seem to flow with the Wood Thrush melody, the future might still hold promise for this often-glorified songbird. As the pioneer farms are slowly abandoned and society learns to value the sanctity of a bird song, the wild spirit of the Wood Thrush offers up an optimistic note.

Similar Species: Hermit Thrush (p. 93) lacks the black spots on the breast and has a reddish rump and tail. Veery (p. 92) and Swainson's Thrush lack the bold black chest spots and reddish head.

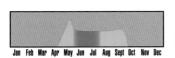

Jan Feb Mar Apr May Jun Jul Aug Sept Oct Nov Dec

Quick I.D.: smaller than a robin; sexes similar; large black spots on white breast; reddish-brown head, rump and tail; white eye ring; plump.
Size: 7¹/₂–8¹/₂ in.

American Robin
Turdus migratorius

If not for its abundance, the American Robin's voice and plumage would inspire pause and praise from casual onlookers. Acclimatization has dealt the robin an unsung hand, however, and it is generally not fully appreciated for the pleasures it offers the eyes and ears of Detroit-area residents. Nevertheless, the American Robin's close relationship with urban areas has allowed many residents an insight into a bird's life. A robin dashing around a yard in search of worms or ripe berries is as familiar to many people as its three-part *cheerily-cheery up-cheerio* song. Michigan's state bird also makes up part of the emotional landscape of communities: their lively song, their spotted young and occasionally even their deaths are experiences shared by their human neighbors.

American Robins appear to be year-round residents in Detroit, but the bird dashing on your lawn in June may not be the same bird that shivers in February among fruiting trees along the Ford test track on Rotunda Drive. Unnoticed by most residents, the neighborhood robins take seasonal shifts: a few new birds arrive from the north just when most of the summer residents depart for southern climes in fall.

Similar Species: Immature robins can be confused with other thrushes, but robins always have at least a hint of red in the breast.

Quick I.D.: smaller than a jay; dark head, back and tail; yellow bill; striped throat; white undertail coverts. *Male:* brick-red breast; darker hood. *Female:* slightly more orange breast; lighter hood.
Size: 9–11 in.

Jan Feb Mar Apr May Jun Jul Aug Sept Oct Nov Dec

BLUEBIRDS & THRUSHES 95

Warbling Vireo
Vireo gilvus

The Warbling Vireo can be quite common during the summer months, but you still need to make a prolonged search before spotting this bird. Lacking any splashy field marks, the Warbling Vireo is exceedingly difficult to spot unless it moves. Searching the tree tops for this inconspicuous bird may be a literal 'pain in the neck,' but the satisfaction in visually confirming its identity can be rewarding.

The velvety voice of the Warbling Vireo contrasts sharply with its dull, nondescript plumage. The often-repeated *I love you, I love you, I love you Ma'am!* song delights the listening forest with its oscillating quality. The phrases finish on an upbeat, as if the bird is asking a question of the wilds.

Similar Species: Red-eyed Vireo (p. 97) has a bold white eyebrow and a gray cap. Tufted Titmouse (p. 86) has a pointed crest and no eyebrow.

breeding

Quick I.D.: smaller than a sparrow; sexes similar; dull white eyebrow; no wing bars; olive-gray upperparts; greenish flanks; light underparts; gray crown.
Size: 4¹/₂–5¹/₂ in.

Jan Feb Mar Apr May Jun Jul Aug Sept Oct Nov Dec

Red-eyed Vireo
Vireo olivaceus

breeding

The Red-eyed Vireo is the undisputed champion of singing endurance. During the breeding season, males sing from tall deciduous trees throughout the day. Most songbirds stop their courting melodies five or six hours after sunrise, but the Red-eyed Vireo seems to gain momentum as the day progresses. One patient ornithologist estimated that the Red-eyed Vireo sings its memorable phrase—*look up, way up, tree top, see me, here-I-am!*—10,000 to 20,000 times a day.

Visual identification of the Red-eyed Vireo is difficult, because its olive-brown color conceals it well among the foliage of deciduous trees. Although this vireo does indeed have red eyes, this feature can only be seen through powerful binoculars in excellent light conditions.

Similar Species: Warbling Vireo (p. 96) lacks the bold white eyebrow and the gray crown.

Quick I.D.: sparrow-sized; sexes similar; gray crown bordered by black; white eyebrow; green back; white underparts; red eyes.
Size: 6 in.

Jan Feb Mar Apr May Jun Jul Aug Sept Oct Nov Dec

Nashville Warbler
Vermivora ruficapilla

This common warbler's name seemed appropriate when Alexander Wilson collected the first specimen in Tennessee, but that original specimen was simply passing through. This misnomer is not an isolated incident, and many other Michigan warblers bear the names given to them during migration: the Cape May (named for a site in New Jersey), Tennessee, Palm and Magnolia warblers are all northern-nesting species.

These cheery and alert-looking birds may not be as boldly splashed with colors as other warblers, but their wardrobe has more permanence: the fall passage sees them in similar dress as in the spring. Nashville Warblers can be easily found fairly low in the shrubs around Metro Beach Metropark, and even in backyards, during their spring and fall migrations.

Similar Species: Common Yellowthroat (p. 110) has a black mask. Yellow Warbler (p. 99) has no gray on its head.

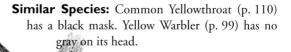

Jan Feb Mar Apr May Jun Jul Aug Sept Oct Nov Dec

Quick I.D.: smaller than a sparrow; sexes similar; yellow underparts, from chin through undertail coverts; pale gray head and face; dark olive back; white eye ring. **Size:** 5 in.

Yellow Warbler
Dendroica petechia

The Yellow Warbler is common in shrublands and in groves of willow and cottonwood. As a consequence of its abundance, it is usually the first warbler birdwatchers identify in their lives—and every spring thereafter. From early May through August, this brilliantly colored warbler is easily found in appropriate habitats throughout our area.

During our winters, Yellow Warblers migrate to the tropics, spending September to April in Mexico and South America. Following the first warm days of spring, the first Yellow Warblers return to our area. Their distinctive courtship song—*sweet-sweet-sweet I'm so-so sweet!*—is easily recognized in early May, despite the bird's eight-month absence. In true warbler fashion, the summertime activities of the Yellow Warbler are energetic and inquisitive: it flits from branch to branch in search of juicy caterpillars, aphids and beetles.

Similar Species: Wilson's Warbler (p. 111) has a small black cap.

Quick I.D.: smaller than a sparrow; yellow overall; darker back, wings and tail; dark eyes and bill. *Male:* bold red streaking on breast. *Female:* often lacks red streaking.
Size: 4–5 in.

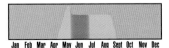

Jan Feb Mar Apr May Jun Jul Aug Sept Oct Nov Dec

Chestnut-sided Warbler
Dendroica pensylvanica

Dropping down to human eye-level, the curious Chestnut-sided Warbler invites all into young deciduous stands with a hearty *so pleased pleased pleased to meet-cha!* greeting. This common woodland warbler appears genuinely hospitable, and in its flitty behavior it often passes within one branch of onlookers. The male's distinctive chestnut and white belly accentuate his brilliance and timeless style for springtime fashion.

Chestnut-sided Warblers are now among the most common warbler migrants to pass through the Detroit area. Young, re-growing forests were far less common before colonization than they are today. Because of this change, it is now possible to see more Chestnut-sided Warblers in a single day than some of the great pioneering naturalists saw in their entire lives.

Similar Species: Male Bay-breasted Warbler (p. 105) lacks the white cheek and throat and has a dark cap. Male Cape May Warbler lacks the white underparts.

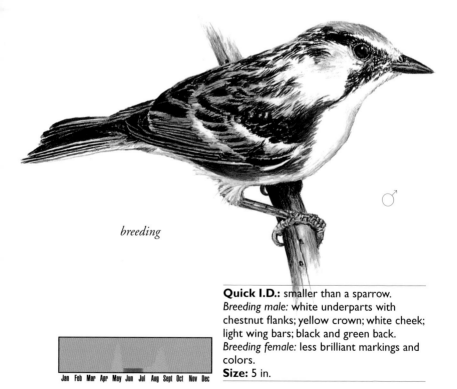

breeding

Quick I.D.: smaller than a sparrow.
Breeding male: white underparts with chestnut flanks; yellow crown; white cheek; light wing bars; black and green back.
Breeding female: less brilliant markings and colors.
Size: 5 in.

Jan Feb Mar Apr May Jun Jul Aug Sept Oct Nov Dec

Magnolia Warbler
Dendroica magnolia

♂

♀

breeding

The Magnolia Warbler is widely regarded as one of the most beautiful wood warblers in North America. Like a customized Cadillac, the Magnolia has all the luxury options—eyebrows, wing bars, a 'necklace,' a yellow rump and breast, tail patches and dark cheeks. As if aware of their stylish beauty, Magnolia Warblers frequently seem to flaunt their colors to birdwatchers at close range. These beautiful warblers can be seen prancing in the low branches and shrubs during migration, as they refuel on newly emerged beetles, flies, wasps and caterpillars.

Birdwatchers have many opportunities to see this glamorous warbler during spring migration at Fairlane Woods, Metro Beach Metropark, William Holliday Park and Kensington Metropark. After a few short weeks in May, however, all Magnolias have left our area in favor of cool spruce and fir forests in northern woods.

Similar Species: Male Yellow-rumped Warbler (p. 102) has a yellow crown and lacks the yellow underparts. Male Cape May Warbler has a rufous cheek.

Quick I.D.: smaller than a sparrow.
Male: yellow underparts with bold black streaks; black mask; white eyebrow; blue-gray crown; dark upperparts; white wing bars. *Female:* duller overall. *In flight:* yellow rump; white tail patches make a nearly complete band across dark tail.
Size: 4¹/₂–5 in.

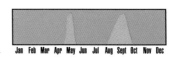

Jan Feb Mar Apr May Jun Jul Aug Sept Oct Nov Dec

Yellow-rumped Warbler
Dendroica coronata

This spirited songbird is as common as it is delightful. Its contrasting colors, curiosity and tinkling trill are enthusiastically admired by even the most jaded birdwatcher. The Yellow-rumped Warbler is the only warbler in the Detroit area that, uncommonly, can be found during winter. It is not during the coldest months, however, that Yellow-rumps are most noticeable; rather it is during April and May, and September and October, when trees in parks and neighborhoods throughout the Detroit area come alive with these colorful birds.

Most experienced birdwatchers call these birds 'Myrtle Warblers.' Until fairly recently, our white-throated form of the Yellow-rumped Warbler was considered a separate species from the western, yellow-throated form. In recognition of the bird's eastern roots and distinct plumage, many birders remain defiant of the name change.

Similar Species: Magnolia Warbler (p. 101) has yellow underparts and white patches in the tail.

Jan Feb Mar Apr May Jun Jul Aug Sept Oct Nov Dec

Quick I.D.: smaller than a sparrow; blue-black back, tail and wings; yellow rump, side patches and crown; white throat; faint white wing bars; dark chest band; white belly; dark cheek. *Male:* bright colors. *Female:* less intense colors.
Size: 5–6 in.

Blackburnian Warbler

Dendroica fusca

In spring, the male Blackburnian Warbler is ablaze with a fiery throat, but it is often this bird's indistinct song that results in detection. Regarded as one of North America's most beautiful warblers, Blackburnians joyfully remain a fairly common migrant through the Detroit area.

Charging up through the central American flyway from wintering grounds in the Andes, these awesomely colored birds arrive in our area around the second week in May. By diverting their routes around the Great Lakes, they funnel through the Detroit area, ornamenting trees like Christmas decorations in Stony Creek Metropark and other parks. The Blackburnian stay is short, however, and within a few weeks all the birds are off to the north. Blackburnian Warblers offer a return engagement in September, but their fall wardrobe is so feeble in comparison to their spring attire that many birders choose to wait until springtime to view them in their celebrated splendor.

Similar Species: American Redstart (p. 108) lacks the orange throat.

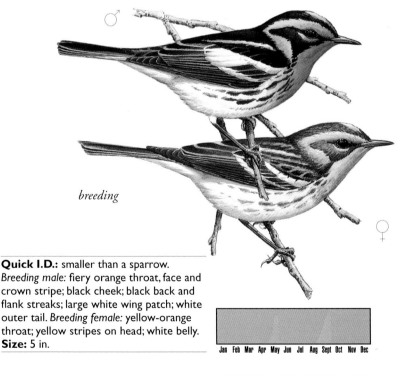

breeding

Quick I.D.: smaller than a sparrow.
Breeding male: fiery orange throat, face and crown stripe; black cheek; black back and flank streaks; large white wing patch; white outer tail. *Breeding female:* yellow-orange throat; yellow stripes on head; white belly.
Size: 5 in.

Jan Feb Mar Apr May Jun Jul Aug Sept Oct Nov Dec

Palm Warbler
Dendroica palmarum

For a few days each spring, Palm Warblers pass through our area to their northern breeding grounds. Palm Warblers are lively transients; they can generally be found low in shrubs or hopping along trails and forest clearings, gleaning for grasshoppers, beetles, moths and flies as comfortably as any sparrow. Their foraging behaviors are surprisingly unique among the wood warblers, which as a group generally go about their foraging in trees and shrubs.

The Palm Warbler's yellow throat gleams surprisingly in sunlight, and the dull red cap strikes a dark contrast. This warbler's most distinctive trait is perhaps its incessant habit of wagging its tail, regardless of whether it is perched or hopping along on the ground. Perhaps this bird should have been named for this wagging feature; it is rarely seen among palms, even on its tropical wintering grounds.

Similar Species: Yellow-rumped Warbler (p. 102) has a yellow rump, darker upperparts and white wing bars. Chipping Sparrow (p. 121) has a stouter body, unstreaked underparts and no yellow in the plumage.

Jan Feb Mar Apr May Jun Jul Aug Sept Oct Nov Dec

Quick I.D.: sparrow-sized; sexes similar; chestnut cap; yellow throat and undertail coverts; streaked brown breast and belly; yellow eyebrows; olive-brown upperparts. **Size:** 5$\frac{1}{2}$ in.

Bay-breasted Warbler
Dendroica castanea

breeding

Bay-breasted Warblers, which visit Detroit-area woods in spring, satisfy the sporting, aesthetic, ecological and scientific objectives of all birdwatchers. Weighing just slightly more than half an ounce, Bay-breasted Warblers amazingly fly a hazard-filled, migratory route between the northern boreal forest and the South American tropics.

Bay-breasted Warblers are splashed with subtle but exquisite hues, which surprise a first-time viewer accustomed to photographic versions of these birds. Spring migrants strain the necks and ears of birders as their thin songs and brief sightings occur at the highest levels of our forests. Bay-breasted Warblers remain in our area only briefly, though; their summer homes lie to the north, where they specialize on clearing forests of spruce budworms.

Similar Species: Cape May Warbler has a red cheek and lacks the reddish flanks and crown. Blackpoll Warbler (p. 106) is streaked black and white.

Quick I.D.: sparrow-sized; cream-colored underparts; two white wing bars. *Breeding male:* chestnut crown, upper breast and flanks; black mask; creamy belly and undertail coverts; cream patch behind ear; two white wing bars. *Female:* pale face, throat and flanks; faint chestnut cap.
Size: 5–6 in.

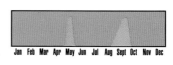

Jan Feb Mar Apr May Jun Jul Aug Sept Oct Nov Dec

Blackpoll Warbler
Dendroica striata

breeding

Blackpolls are the champion migrants among the warblers. Weighing less than two 25-cent coins, these warblers pass through Michigan on their way between South America and their breeding grounds in northern Canada and Alaska. Unlike other warblers, which choose a landlocked migratory passage, Blackpolls shortcut their journey by flying south over the Atlantic Ocean, leaving land at Cape Cod and not landing again until they reach the coast of Venezuela.

Although Blackpolls may not be as numerous during their spring passage, their bold breeding plumage allows for much easier identification. They pass through our area quite commonly at this time of year, but their activities are infrequently noticed because they generally fly at night and forage in treetops. When cold weather and rains strike Detroit in mid-May, Blackpoll Warblers are often grounded in Fairlane Woods, impatiently waiting in the trees for the weather to turn bright.

Similar Species: Black-and-white Warbler (p. 107) has dark legs and a striped, black-and-white crown. Black-capped Chickadee (p. 85) has a black bib and dark legs and lacks the streaks on its flanks.

Jan Feb Mar Apr May Jun Jul Aug Sept Oct Nov Dec

Quick I.D.: sparrow-sized; two white wing bars; orange legs. *Breeding male:* black cap and upperparts; white cheek; black-streaked underparts. *Breeding female:* streaked, greenish upperparts; black-streaked or white underparts; dirty cheek. **Size:** 5 1/2 in.

Black-and-white Warbler
Mniotilta varia

The foraging behavior of the Black-and-white Warbler lies in sharp contrast to most of its kin. Rather than dancing quickly between twig perches like most warblers, Black-and-white Warblers have a foraging strategy similar to an entirely unrelated group of birds—the nuthatches. As if possessed by nuthatch envy, Black-and-white Warblers hop gingerly up and down tree trunks in search of insect eggs, larval insects, beetles, spiders and other invertebrates.

Black-and-white Warblers occur regularly throughout our area in migration, appearing in backyards and at William Holliday Park, Metro Beach Metropark and Stony Creek Metropark during their prolonged spring and fall passages. A novice birdwatcher can easily identify this two-toned and oddly behaved warbler. A keen ear also helps: the gentle oscillating song—like a wheel in need of greasing—is easily identified and remembered.

Similar Species: Blackpoll Warbler (p. 106) has orange legs and a solid black cap.

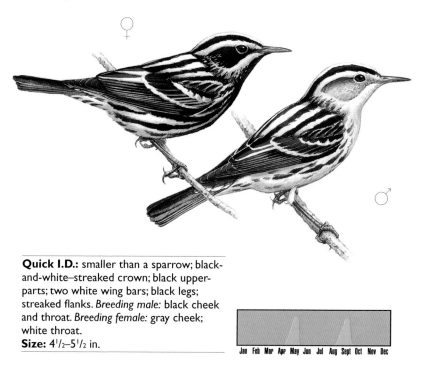

Quick I.D.: smaller than a sparrow; black-and-white–streaked crown; black upperparts; two white wing bars; black legs; streaked flanks. *Breeding male:* black cheek and throat. *Breeding female:* gray cheek; white throat.
Size: 4¹/₂–5¹/₂ in.

Jan Feb Mar Apr May Jun Jul Aug Sept Oct Nov Dec

American Redstart
Setophaga ruticilla

Like an over-energized wind-up toy, the American Redstart flits from branch to branch in a dizzying pursuit of prey. Never for a moment will a redstart pause. Even while it is perched, its orange-splashed tail waves gently behind it. This erratic and amusing behavior is easily observed on this bird's summering ground, as well as in its Central American wintering habitat, where it is affectionately known as *candelita* (the little candle). With constantly quivering wings, tail and shoulders, the Redstart's patches are sparks of life in any dark forest.

Although American Redstarts are one of the most common warblers to pass through the Detroit area, their songs are so wonderfully various that even after a spring season spent listening to them, their songs can still be confusing. During May and June, take a walk through a deciduous forest to discover this bird's energy and enthusiasm.

Similar Species: Blackburnian Warbler (p. 103) has an orange throat and face and lacks the orange patches in the wings and tail. Red-winged Blackbird (p. 131) is much larger, with no red on its chest or tail.

Quick I.D.: smaller than a sparrow. *Male:* black overall with fiery orange patches in wings, tail and side of breast; white belly. *Female:* olive-brown back; light underparts; peach-yellow patches in wings and tail and on shoulders. **Size:** 5 in.

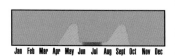

Jan Feb Mar Apr May Jun Jul Aug Sept Oct Nov Dec

Ovenbird
Seiurus aurocapillus

The Ovenbird—or at least its song, *teacher teacher Teacher TEACHER!*— is encountered frequently. Its loud and distinctive song announces its presence in mature deciduous woods, and its noisy habit of running through the undergrowth nearly reveals its precise location. Despite having a good indication of the Ovenbird's location, this songbird's cryptic plumage and refusal to become airborne frustrate many birders intent on a quick peek. Rarely will Ovenbirds expose themselves to the open forest; they seem most comfortable in the tangles of shrubs, stumps and dead leaves.

The sharp, loud call of the Ovenbird rises from the dense layer of shrubs and plants and is one of the most distinctive voices of Detroit-area forests. Unfortunately, our disappearing mature deciduous forests have also taken a toll on this special bird, because they are continually yielding their forest patches to development.

Similar Species: Hermit Thrush (p. 93) and Wood Thrush (p. 94) are much larger, and they lack the streaked russet crown. Northern Water-thrush lacks the russet crown and has a white eyebrow.

Quick I.D.: sparrow-sized; sexes similar; heavily streaked breast; bold eye ring; olive-brown back; russet crown bordered by black; orange legs.
Size: 6 in.

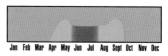

Jan Feb Mar Apr May Jun Jul Aug Sept Oct Nov Dec

Common Yellowthroat
Geothlypis trichas

With so much diversity within North America's wood warbler clan, it is no surprise that one species has forsaken forests in favor of cattail marshes. In our area, this energetic warbler reaches its highest abundance along wetland brambles and cattails, but it can be seen and heard along the vegetation bordering many freshwater bodies or even in fields that are not even wet.

The male Common Yellowthroat is easily identified by his black mask or by his oscillating *witchety-witchety-witchety!* song. Female yellowthroats are rarely seen because they keep to their nests, deep within the thick vegetation surrounding marshes. The three to five young hatch after only about 12 days of incubation. These young continue their rapid development, soon leaving the nest, allowing the parents to raise a second brood. Common Yellowthroat nests are often parasitized by Brown-headed Cowbirds.

Similar Species: Male is distinct. Nashville Warbler (p. 98) has dark brown legs and an eye ring. Female Wilson's Warbler (p. 111) has a yellow eyebrow and hint of a dark cap.

Quick I.D.: smaller than a sparrow; orange legs; yellow throat and underparts; olive upperparts. *Male:* black mask, with white border on forehead. *Female:* no mask.

Size: 4¹/₂–5¹/₂ in.

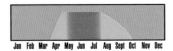

Jan Feb Mar Apr May Jun Jul Aug Sept Oct Nov Dec

Wilson's Warbler
Wilsonia pusilla

♀

♂

The descending trill of the Wilson's
Warbler reveals the presence of this small, colorful
bird. In classic warbler style, it feeds energetically on
caterpillars and other·insects in branches that are low to the
ground, often near water. Often flitting to within a branch of onlookers,
this energetic warbler bounces from one perch to another like an over-
wound wind-up toy.

This warbler was named for Alexander Wilson, the father of American
ornithology. During its spring and fall migrations, the Wilson's Warbler
can be found almost anywhere in our area. During the nesting season,
however, this bird chooses nesting grounds in northern Michigan and
Canada.

Similar Species: Yellow Warbler (p. 99) has a streaked breast and lacks
the black cap.

Quick I.D.: smaller than a sparrow;
lemon- yellow underparts; olive to dark
green upperparts. *Male:* black cap.
Female: much duller cap; hint of yellow
eyebrow.
Size: 5 in.

Jan Feb Mar Apr May Jun Jul Aug Sept Oct Nov Dec

Canada Warbler
Wilsonia canadensis

♀

♂

breeding

Male Canada Warblers have a wide-eyed and alert appearance with their bold, white eye rings. These warblers are sometimes inquisitive; they might pop up from dense deciduous shrubs in response to intrusive hikers. At eye level, they can occasionally be seen through leafing out branches, singing out their lively song, the distinctiveness of which lies in its loose notes and unpatterned rhythm.

Although several wood warblers breed almost exclusively in Canada, this species isn't one of them. Canada Warblers also breed throughout the northern parts of Michigan and as close to Detroit as Tuscola County. Like so many of the migrants that pass through our area, the time Canada Warblers spend here seems far too fleeting. Although birders may satisfy themselves with a glimpse or two of these birds, the feeling is short-lived, motivating them once again in the spring to catch up with Canada Warblers in passage.

Similar Species: Male Magnolia Warbler (p. 101) has white wing bars, a yellow rump, a black mask and a white eye ring. Male Yellow-rumped Warbler (p. 102) has a yellow rump, white wing patches and a white belly. Kirtland's Warbler lacks the yellow spectacles and has wing bars.

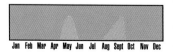

Jan Feb Mar Apr May Jun Jul Aug Sept Oct Nov Dec

Quick I.D.: small sparrow–sized; pale yellow 'spectacles'; yellow underparts; dark upperparts; orange legs; white undertail coverts. *Breeding male:* blue-black back; dark 'necklace.' *Female:* blue-green back; faint 'necklace.'
Size: 5–5¹/₂ in.

Scarlet Tanager
Piranga olivacea

The tropical appearance of the male Scarlet Tanager's plumage reinforces the link between the forests of South America and eastern North America. A winter resident of the tropics and a breeder in Detroit's mature deciduous woods, this tanager is vulnerable to deforestation at both extremes of its range.

Scarlet Tanagers can be difficult to see, despite their tropical wardrobe, because they tend to stay high up in forest canopies. They sing a robin-like warble—*hurry-worry-lurry-scurry!*—that is frequently disregarded as coming from that more familiar woodland voice. Novice birdwatchers should listen for the tanager's hiccup-like *chick-burr* call as it cascades to the forest floor. This tanager occasionally forages close to the ground in rainy weather.

The Scarlet Tanager is one of Detroit's most beautiful birds, and every brief encounter is sure to make you wish that the meeting might have lasted just a little longer.

Similar Species: Northern Cardinal (p. 139) has a crest and a heavy bill and lacks the black wings. Baltimore Oriole (p. 135) and Orchard Oriole both lack the combination of an all-red body and black wings.

breeding

Quick I.D.: larger than a sparrow.
Male: unmistakable, magnificent scarlet body with contrasting black wings and tail; changes in the fall to look like female.
Female: olive-yellow overall.
Size: 6¹/₂–7¹/₂ in.

Jan Feb Mar Apr May Jun Jul Aug Sept Oct Nov Dec

Horned Lark
Eremophila alpestris

Horned Larks are probably most frequently encountered as they rise up in front of vehicles speeding along country roads. Larks cut off to the side of cars an instant before a fatal collision, briefly showing off their distinct black tail. Horned Larks resort to these near misses because their first instinct when threatened is to outrun their pursuer. Cars easily overtake these swift runners, so larks take to the air when their first attempt to flee fails.

Late winter is the best season to observe these open country specialists. They congregate in flocks on outlying farm fields, eating waste grain. Most of these birds are destined to migrate north when the first hints of warmth loosen winter's chilly grip, but this does not mean that our area is free of these birds through summer, because a few nest in the open fields and pastures that have not yet fallen to urbanization. Horned Larks are among the earliest of our courting birds, singing their songs and diving dare-devilishly before the snow has all retreated.

Similar Species: Sparrows lack the black facial and throat markings.

♂

Quick I.D.: larger than a sparrow; brown plumage; black bib, mask and 'tiara'; light underparts; white outer tail feathers; faint yellow throat. *Female:* duller overall; less prominent 'horns.'
Size: 7–8 in.

Gray Catbird
Dumetella carolinensis

The Gray Catbird is a sleek bird that commonly displays an unusual 'mooning' behavior—it raises its long, slender tail to show its chestnut undertail coverts. This behavior is one of the elements of courtship, and the coverts may help female catbirds to choose the best mates.

The Gray Catbird is a bird of dense shrubs and thickets, and although it's relatively common in appropriate habitats, its distinctive call, rather than the bird itself, is what is most commonly encountered. The Gray Catbird's unmistakable cat-like 'meowing,' for which it's named, can be heard rising from shrubs at the University of Michigan–Dearborn during May and June.

Similar Species: None.

Quick I.D.: smaller than a robin; sexes similar; slate gray; black cap; chestnut undertail coverts; long, dark tail.
Size: 9 in.

Jan Feb Mar Apr May Jun Jul Aug Sept Oct Nov Dec

Brown Thrasher
Toxostoma rufum

Male Brown Thrashers have the largest vocal repertoire of any Detroit-area bird—more than 3000 song types. Although thrashers don't have the sweetest voices in Detroit, their loud, continually varying songs are worth a listen. Thrashers will repeat phrases twice, often combining them into complex choruses, such as *dig-it dig-it, hoe-it hoe-it, pull-it-up pull-it-up.*

Brown Thrashers have a reddish-brown back and tail and a heavily streaked breast. They're found in the sparse patches of thickets and shrubs, often in close proximity to humans. They're shy birds, however, and they need a lot of coaxing with squeaks and pishes before they pop out into the open. In summer, Oakwoods Metropark offers an opportunity to meet this dynamic songster.

Similar Species: Wood Thrush (p. 94) and Veery (p. 92) both have shorter tails and straight bills.

Jan Feb Mar Apr May Jun Jul Aug Sept Oct Nov Dec

Quick I.D.: jay-sized; sexes similar; reddish-brown head, back and tail; heavy chest streaking; long, downcurved bill; white wing bars; long tail; no eye ring.
Size: 11–12 in.

Cedar Waxwing
Bombycilla cedrorum

A faint, high-pitched trill is often your first clue that waxwings are around. Search the treetops to see these cinnamon-crested birds as they dart out in quick bursts, snacking on flying insects. Cedar Waxwings are found in many habitats throughout Detroit, wherever ripe berries provide abundant food supplies.

Cedar Waxwings are most often seen in large flocks in late spring and fall, when they congregate on fruit trees and quickly eat all the berries. Some people remember these visits not only for the birds' beauty, but because fermentation of the fruit occasionally renders the flock flightless from intoxication.

Similar Species: Tufted Titmouse (p. 86) has no yellow on its belly or tail.

Quick I.D.: smaller than a robin; sexes similar; fine, pale, silky-brown plumage; small crest; black mask; yellow belly wash; yellow-tipped tail; light undertail coverts; shiny red (waxy-looking) droplets on wing tips.
Size: 7–8 in.

Jan Feb Mar Apr May Jun Jul Aug Sept Oct Nov Dec

European Starling
Sturnus vulgaris

In 1924, 34 years after their intentional release in New York's Central Park, European Starlings began to establish themselves in Michigan. Less than a decade later, flocks of over one million birds were being reported. Today, European Starlings are one of the most common birds in Detroit. Their presence is highlighted by astonishing numbers roosting communally under the Ambassador Bridge during the winter months.

Unfortunately, the expansion of starlings has come at the expense of many of our native birds, including the Purple Martin and the Eastern Bluebird, which are unable to defend their nest cavities against the aggressive starlings. Few birdwatchers are pleased with the presence of this foreigner to our area, but starlings have become a permanent fixture in the bird community. If residents are unable to find joy in this bird's mimicry and flocking, they may take some comfort from the fact that starlings now provide a reliable and stable food source for woodland hawks and the downtown's Peregrine Falcons.

Similar Species: All blackbirds have longer tails and black bills. Purple Martin (p. 80) has a short bill.

breeding

Quick I.D.: smaller than a robin; sexes similar; short tail. *Breeding:* dark, glossy plumage; long, yellow bill. *Non-breeding:* dark bill; spotty plumage. *Juvenile:* brown upperparts; gray-brown underparts; brown bill. **Size:** 8–9 in.

Jan Feb Mar Apr May Jun Jul Aug Sept Oct Nov Dec

Eastern Towhee
Pipilo erythrophthalmus

This large, cocky sparrow is most often heard before it is seen scratching away leaves and debris under dense shrubs and bushes. It is a summer resident in Detroit-area shrubby fields, such as Pontiac Lake State Recreation Area. Deep in the shadows of shrubs, the Eastern Towhee's sharp *Drink your Teeea* identifies this secretive sparrow.

To best observe this bird, which was formerly grouped with the West's Spotted Towhee (together they were known as the Rufous-sided Towhee), learn a few birding tricks. Squeaking and pishing are irresistible sounds for towhees; soon they will pop out from cover to investigate the curious noise.

Similar Species: American Robin (p. 95) is larger and has no white on its chest. Dark-eyed Junco (p. 129) is smaller and has white outer tail feathers.

Quick I.D.: smaller than a robin; black head; rufous-colored flanks; black back; white outer tail feathers; white underparts; red eyes. *Male:* black head, breast and upperparts. *Female:* brown head, breast and upperparts.
Size: 8–9 in.

Jan Feb Mar Apr May Jun Jul Aug Sept Oct Nov Dec

American Tree Sparrow

Spizella arborea

The American Tree Sparrow's annual flood into Michigan during late fall is a sign of the changing seasons. For the entire winter, these arctic nesters decorate the leafless rural shrublands like ornaments on a Christmas tree. As a regular arrival in late October and as one of the first songbirds to disappear in April, the American Tree Sparrow quietly announces the closing of fall and the opening of spring.

These humble, quiet sparrows often go unnoticed despite their large numbers. American Tree Sparrows often visit suburban feeders during their migrations and while wintering in the Detroit area, but they never attempt to usurp the surly resident flocks of House Sparrows and House Finches.

Similar Species: Chipping Sparrow (p. 121), Field Sparrow (p. 122) and Swamp Sparrow (p. 126) all lack the breast spot.

non-breeding

Quick I.D.: large sparrow; sexes similar; red crown; no eyebrow; small central chest spot on otherwise unstreaked breast; mottled back.
Size: 6 in.

Jan Feb Mar Apr May Jun Jul Aug Sept Oct Nov Dec

Chipping Sparrow
Spizella passerina

breeding

Hopping around freshly mowed lawns, the cheery Chipping Sparrow goes about its business unconcerned by the busy world of suburban Detroit. One of Michigan's most widespread species, the Chipping Sparrow brings birdwatching to those who rarely venture from their homes.

These sparrows nest frequently in our backyards, building their small nest cups with dried vegetation and lining them with animal hair. Chipping Sparrows usually attempt to bring up two broods of young every year in Detroit. Three or four small, greenish-blue eggs are laid in mid-May, and later near the beginning of July, should conditions prove favorable. These passive birds are delightful neighbors in our backyards, and they demand nothing more than a little privacy around an ornamental conifer where they have chosen to nest.

Similar Species: American Tree Sparrow (p. 120) is only a winter resident and has a black central chest spot. Swamp Sparrow (p. 126) lacks the clean white, black-lined eyebrow. Field Sparrow (p. 122) has a pink bill and lacks the white eyebrow.

Quick I.D.: small sparrow; sexes similar; red crown; white eyebrow; black eye line; clear grayish breast; mottled back.
Size: 5¹/₂ in.

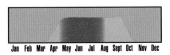

Jan Feb Mar Apr May Jun Jul Aug Sept Oct Nov Dec

Field Sparrow
Spizella pusilla

The innocent, unmarked face of the Field Sparrow gives this common bird a perpetual look of adolescence. Like a teenager prior to his first shave, the Field Sparrow has a soft, wholesome look, highlighted by its pink bill and untainted eye.

Many sparrows have very descriptive and accurate names, but the Field Sparrow's name is somewhat misleading. An inhabitant of overgrown meadows and bushy areas, Field Sparrows tend to avoid open, expansive, grassy fields. Their nesting sites are often found away from developments, but not far enough from Brown-headed Cowbirds. These nest parasites may occupy over one-quarter of the nests in our area, affecting this sparrow's reproductive success. Fortunately, cowbirds have not significantly decreased the population of these tireless singers, who offer their voices on hot summer days when most other singers are quiet.

Similar Species: Chipping Sparrow (p. 121) has a white eyebrow and a black eye line. American Tree Sparrow (p. 120) has a dark chest spot and a dark bill.

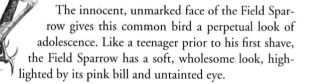

Quick I.D.: mid-sized sparrow; sexes similar; reddish crown; plain gray underparts; pink bill; light gray eyebrow; rusty brown back.
Size: 5–6 in.

Jan Feb Mar Apr May Jun Jul Aug Sept Oct Nov Dec

Savannah Sparrow
Passerculus sandwichensis

The Savannah Sparrow is a common bird of the open country. Its dull brown plumage and streaked breast conceal it perfectly in the long grasses of native prairies, farms and roadsides. It breeds in fields of weedy annuals and grasses at many local parks.

The Savannah Sparrow resorts to flight only as a last alternative—it prefers to run swiftly and inconspicuously through long grass—and it is most often seen darting across roads and open fields. Its dull brown plumage and streaked breast conceal it perfectly in the long grasses of meadows, farms and roadsides. The Savannah Sparrow's distinctive buzzy trill—*tea-tea-tea-teeea today*—and the yellow patch in front of its eye are the best ways to distinguish it from the other grassland sparrows.

Similar Species: Song Sparrow (p. 125) has a prominent breast spot and no yellow on the face.

Quick I.D.: small sparrow; sexes similar; streaked underparts and upperparts; mottled brown above; dark cheek; no white outer tail feathers; many have yellow lore.
Size: 5–6 in.

Jan Feb Mar Apr May Jun Jul Aug Sept Oct Nov Dec

Fox Sparrow
Passerella iliaca

Most of the migrant birds in our area require a bit of effort to see them during their passage, but a well-stocked backyard feeder may be all that is required to see a Fox Sparrow. During April and then again in late September and October, Fox Sparrows pass through the Detroit area, feeding at the finest feeders offered by local residents.

Fox Sparrows are generally easy for the backyard naturalist to identify, because they are not here long enough to become familiar. They follow the general sparrow body plan, but they are more stocky, like a linebacker. They hop about on the ground, picking up fallen seeds, but they never flash any sign of color. Rather, it is their lack of splendid color that finally confirms the identity of these Canadian breeders; their boldly streaked breast and neat, dark back set them apart from the backyard crowd

Similar Species: Song Sparrow (p. 125) has a different song and is much lighter in color. Hermit Thrush (p. 93) has a smaller bill and thinner breast spots. Swainson's Thrush has a pale eye ring and olive upperparts.

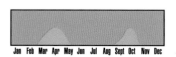

Jan Feb Mar Apr May Jun Jul Aug Sept Oct Nov Dec

Quick I.D.: large sparrow; sexes similar; heavy breast streaks form dark chest; gray-brown with reddish tail and reddish-brown breast spots.
Size: 6¹/₂–7 in.

Song Sparrow
Melospiza melodia

The Song Sparrow's drab, heavily streaked plumage doesn't prepare you for its symphonic song, which stands among the best in the Detroit area for complexity and rhythm. This commonly heard bird seems to be singing *hip-hip-hip hooray boys, the spring is here again.*

This year-round resident is encountered in a wide variety of habitats: Song Sparrows are easily found all spring and summer among marshes, thickets, brambles, weedy fields and woodland edges. During winter, most birds withdraw, but a few can be encountered at feeders and at Oakwoods Metropark and Belle Isle.

Although Song Sparrows are most easily identified by their grayish facial streaks while they are perched, flying birds will characteristically pump their tails.

Similar Species: Fox Sparrow (p. 124) is very heavily streaked and has a different song. Savannah Sparrow (p. 123) and Lincoln's Sparrow have weaker breast streaks.

Quick I.D.: mid-sized sparrow; sexes similar; heavy breast streaks form central spot; brown plumage; striped head.
Size: 6–7 in.

Jan Feb Mar Apr May Jun Jul Aug Sept Oct Nov Dec

Swamp Sparrow
Melospiza georgiana

breeding

Although Swamp Sparrows are fairly common in wetlands in the Detroit area, such as at Metro Beach Metropark, they are far less visible than their neighbors, the blackbirds and yellowthroats. Except when the male pounces atop a bulrush or willow branch to sing his sweet, loose trill, Swamp Sparrows seem perfectly content to remain hidden deep within the world of cattails and grasses. They can be readily enticed to quickly pop up to a cattail head, however, in response to a birder's urging squeaks.

Of the sparrows in our area, Swamp Sparrows are the most adapted to life around water. Like all other sparrows, they are unable to swim, but that fact is no deterrent to this rufous-crowned skulker. Swamp Sparrows glean much of their insectivorous diet directly from the surface of wetlands, and they construct their sideways nest just a foot above the water line.

Similar Species: Breeding Chipping Sparrow (p. 121) has clean white eyebrows, black eye line and uniform gray underparts. American Tree Sparrow (p. 120) has a central dark chest spot and a two-toned bill. Song Sparrow (p. 125) has a heavily streaked chest with a central breast spot.

Quick I.D.: mid-sized sparrow; sexes similar; gray face; rufous shoulders; streaked back. *Breeding:* red cap; white throat; light gray breast; reddish-brown underparts. *Non-breeding:* streaked, brown cap.
Size: 5½ in.

Jan Feb Mar Apr May Jun Jul Aug Sept Oct Nov Dec

White-throated Sparrow
Zonotrichia albicollis

The catchy song of the White-throated Sparrow is often on the lips of weekend cottagers returning from the north country. By whistling the distinctive *Old Sam Peabody Peabody Peabody* to themselves, people bring some of the atmosphere of the northern woods home to the city. The voice of conifer woods is as sure a sign of spring in cottage country as the melting snow and returning cottagers.

In winter, a few White-throated Sparrows migrate to Belle Isle, where birdfeeders provide them with a steady supply of seed without much physical exertion. Its striped head and white throat allow this forest breeder to stand out from other sparrows and from House Finches.

Similar Species: White-crowned Sparrow (p. 128) lacks the white throat and has a pink bill.

white-striped phase

Quick I.D.: large sparrow; sexes similar; black-and-white–striped head; white throat; unstreaked, light gray breast; yellow lore; rusty-brown upperparts; tan morph has brownish, rather than white, streaks on head.
Size: 6¹/₂–7 in.

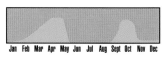

Jan Feb Mar Apr May Jun Jul Aug Sept Oct Nov Dec

White-crowned Sparrow
Zonotrichia leucophrys

During May and October, migrating White-crowned Sparrows are usually seen foraging on the ground or in low shrubs. They normally feed a short distance from thickets and tall grasses, always maintaining a quick escape path into the safety of concealing vegetation. During winter, White-crowned Sparrows often feed at backyard feeders in rural areas.

Prior to their spring departure, White-throated Sparrows please the Detroit area with their distinctive *I-I-I-I gotto go wee wee wee now* song. It is freely offered at regular intervals from the tops of bushes or other perches. The sparrow arches its head way back, opens its bill and sings from the bottom of its heart.

Similar Species: White-throated Sparrow (p. 127) has a yellow lore and a clear white throat.

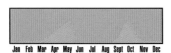

Jan Feb Mar Apr May Jun Jul Aug Sept Oct Nov Dec

Quick I.D.: large sparrow; sexes similar; striped, black-and-white crown; pink bill; unstreaked breast; brown upperparts; gray-brown underparts. *Immature:* no crown; buffy-olive upperparts; faint buffy underparts.
Size: 5¹/₂–7 in.

Dark-eyed Junco
Junco hyemalis

Dark-eyed Juncos occur as abundant winter visitors throughout the Detroit area. The Dark-eyed Junco is a ground dweller, and it is frequently seen as it flushes from the undergrowth along wooded trails in Detroit's parks. The distinctive, white outer tail feathers flash in alarm as it flies down a narrow path before disappearing into a thicket.

Just before departing for their northern breeding grounds in early April, Dark-eyed Juncos sing their descending trills, which are easily mistaken with those of the Chipping Sparrow. The junco's distinctive smacking call and its habit of double-scratching at forest litter also help identify it. Juncos are frequent guests at birdfeeders throughout Detroit, usually cleaning up the scraps that have fallen to the ground.

Similar Species: Eastern Towhee (p. 119) is larger and has conspicuous rufous sides. Brown-headed Cowbird (p. 134) lacks the white outer tail feathers and the white belly.

Quick I.D.: large sparrow; slate gray; light-colored bill; white outer tail feathers; white belly. *Female:* somewhat duller.
Size: 5–6¹/₂ in.

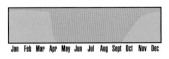

Bobolink
Dolichonyx oryzivorus

breeding

During spring, small flocks of Bobolinks return to weedy fields in our area to grace cool mornings with their songs. The males arrive a few days before the females and perform their bubbly, tinkly song, *bob-o-link bob-o-link, spink, spank, spink,* assuring farmers and naturalists that spring is here to stay.

At first glimpse, Bobolinks look every bit a sparrow, especially the drab females, which lack the male's style—looking as though he's wearing a tuxedo backwards. But these are not sparrows at all, but blackbirds—evident by their polygynous breeding strategy. Males that acquire prime hayfields might mate and defend several nesting females.

The fall migration of Bobolinks is one of the most spectacular and longest of all songbirds. flocks leaving Michigan congregate with others farther south and soon number in the thousands. These flocks once descended on rice crops in the Southeast, and they were known as 'rice birds' for this destructive practice.

Similar Species: Brown-headed Cowbird (p. 134) has a black back. Sparrows tend to lack the pointy tail feathers.

Jan Feb Mar Apr May Jun Jul Aug Sept Oct Nov Dec

Quick I.D.: larger than a sparrow; pointed tail feathers. *Breeding male:* black head and body; buffy nape; white rump. *Female and Non-breeding male:* buffy brown body; dark crown streaks; dark eye line.
Size: 6–8 in.

Red-winged Blackbird
Agelaius phoeniceus

From March through July, no marsh is free from the loud calls and bossy, aggressive nature of the Red-winged Blackbird. A springtime walk around Oakwoods Metropark or through the brush at any wetland or field will be accompanied by this bird's loud, raspy and persistent *konk-a-reee* or *eat my CHEEEzies* song.

♂

♀

The male's bright red shoulders are his most important tool in the strategic and intricate displays he uses to defend his territory from rivals and to attract a mate. In experiments, males whose red shoulders were painted black soon lost their territories to rivals they had previously defeated. The female's interest lies not in the individual combatants, however, but in the nesting habitat, and a male who can successfully defend a large area of dense cattails will breed with many females. After the females have built their concealed nests and laid their eggs, the male continues his persistent vigil.

Similar Species: Brown-headed Cowbird (p. 134) and Common Grackle (p. 133) both lack the red shoulder patches.

Quick I.D.: smaller than a robin. *Male:* all-black plumage; large red patch bordered by creamy yellow on each shoulder. *Female:* brown overall; heavily streaked; hint of red on shoulder.
Size: 7¹/₂–9¹/₂ in.

Jan Feb Mar Apr May Jun Jul Aug Sept Oct Nov Dec

Eastern Meadowlark
Sturnella magna

The Eastern Meadowlark is well adapted to the landscape of fields and pastures where it spends its summers. Its flute-like song, *This is the Year,* is a signature of open country, such as Oakwoods Metropark.

Eastern Meadowlarks are both showy and perfectly camouflaged. Their yellow sweater with the black V-neck and their white outer tail feathers serve to attract mates. Potential meadowlark mates face one another, raise their bills high and perform a grassland ballet. Oddly, the colorful breast and white tail feathers are also used to attract the attention of potential predators. Foxes, hawks or falcons focus on these bold features in pursuit, but then their prey mysteriously disappears into the grass whenever the meadowlark chooses to turn its back or fold away its white tail flags.

Similar Species: None, except where its range overlaps with the Western Meadowlark.

breeding

Quick I.D.: robin-sized; sexes similar; mottled brown upperparts; black 'V' on chest; yellow throat and belly; white outer tail feathers; striped head.
Size: 8–10 in.

Jan Feb Mar Apr May Jun Jul Aug Sept Oct Nov Dec

Common Grackle

Quiscalus quiscula

The Common Grackle is a noisy and cocky bird that prefers to feed on the ground in open areas. Birdfeeders in rural areas can attract large numbers of these blackish birds, whose cranky disposition drives away most other birds (even quarrelsome Blue Jays and House Sparrows). The Common Grackle is easily identified by its long tail, large bill and dark plumage, which can shine with hues of green, purple and blue in bright light.

The Common Grackle is a poor but spirited singer. Usually while perched in a shrub, a male grackle will slowly take a deep breath that inflates his chest and causes his feathers to rise. Then he closes his eyes and gives out a loud, surprising *swaaaack*, not unlike a rusty gate. Despite our perception of the Common Grackle's musical weakness, following his 'song,' the male smugly and proudly poses with his bill held high.

Similar Species: Red-winged Blackbird (p. 131) and Brown-headed Cowbird (p. 134) have relatively shorter tails and dark eyes. American Crow (p. 84) is much larger.

Quick I.D.: jay-sized; sexes similar; glossy black plumage with purple and bronze iridescence; long tail; yellow eyes; large bill. **Size:** 11–13 in.

Jan Feb Mar Apr May Jun Jul Aug Sept Oct Nov Dec

Brown-headed Cowbird
Molothrus ater

Since it first arrived Michigan in 1850, the Brown-headed Cowbird has firmly established itself within the matrix of the region's bird life. This gregarious bird is very common in outlying agricultural areas, and it can be seen anywhere.

The Brown-headed Cowbird is infamous for being a nest parasite. Female cowbirds do not incubate their own eggs, but instead lay them in the nests of many songbirds. Cowbird eggs have a short incubation period, and the cowbird chicks often hatch before the host songbird's own chicks. Many songbirds will continue to feed the fast-growing cowbird chick even after the it has outgrown its surrogate parent. In its efforts to get as much food as possible, a cowbird chick may squeeze the host's own young out of the nest. The populations of some songbirds have been reduced in part by the activities of the Brown-headed Cowbird, but other songbird species recognize the foreign egg, and they either eject it from their nest or they build a new nest.

Similar Species: Common Grackle (p. 133) has a long tail and yellow eyes.

Quick I.D.: smaller than a robin.
Male: metallic-looking, glossy black plumage; soft brown head; dark eyes.
Female: brownish gray overall; dark eyes; slight chest streaks.
Size: 6–8 in.

Jan Feb Mar Apr May Jun Jul Aug Sept Oct Nov Dec

Baltimore Oriole
Icterus galbula

♂

♀

Although it is a common summer resident of city parks and woodlands, the Baltimore Oriole is seldom seen. Unlike the American Robin, which inhabits the human domain of shrubs and lawns, the Baltimore Oriole nests and feeds in the tallest deciduous trees available. The vacant nest, which is easily seen on bare trees in fall, is often the only indication that a pair of orioles summered in an area. This bird's hanging, six-inch-deep, pouch-like nest is deceptively strong.

The male Baltimore Oriole's striking, Halloween-like, black-and-orange plumage flashes like embers amidst the dense foliage of the treetops, while its slow, purposeful *Peter Peter here here Peter Peter* song drips to the forest floor.

From mid-May to mid-July, deciduous forests at Fairlane Woods and backroads in Oakland County are among the most productive destinations for oriole-starved Detroit-area birdwatchers.

Similar Species: Orchard Oriole is smaller and has chestnut, rather than orange, plumage.

Quick I.D.: smaller than a robin.
Male: brilliant orange belly flanks, outer tail feathers and rump; black hood, wings and tail. *Female:* yellow-green upperparts; yellow throat; faint hood.
Size: 7–8 in.

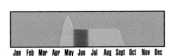

Jan Feb Mar Apr May Jun Jul Aug Sept Oct Nov Dec

Purple Finch
Carpodacus purpureus

The Purple Finch breeds throughout northern Michigan, but it is most often seen at winter feeders in the Detroit area. Purple Finches are a blessing to see on cold winter days; their raspberry plumage differs slightly from that of the more common House Finches. Their numbers vary from year to year, and they can be common in certain neighborhoods. Prior to the bird's departure, the liquid warbling song of the males bubbles through the treetops.

Their gentle nature and the simple, but stunning, plumage of the male are endearing features, but the Purple Finch's habit of offering its voice to the crisp winter air is what is most appreciated by its human audience.

Similar Species: Male House Finch (p. 137) has a darker red breast and eyebrow, a streaked belly and streaked undertail coverts. Female Rose-breasted Grosbeak (p. 140) is larger and has white wing bars.

Quick I.D.: sparrow-sized; notched tail. *Male:* raspberry head, nape, throat and rump; reddish-brown cheek; streaked back; white undertail coverts. *Female:* brown overall; streaked underparts; white eyebrow; prominent whisker (mustache); brown cheeks.
Size: 5¹/₂ in.

IRREGULAR

Jan Feb Mar Apr May Jun Jul Aug Sept Oct Nov Dec

House Finch
Carpodacus mexicanus

The House Finch is one of the earliest voices to announce the coming of spring. These common city and country birds sing their melodies from backyards, parks, ivy vines and telephone lines.

During the 1920s and 1930s, these birds, native to the American Southwest, were popular cage birds, and they were sold across the continent as Hollywood finches. Illegal releases of the caged birds and expansion from their historic range have resulted in two separate distributions in North America, which have recently converged. If your backyard feeder continues to remain free of House Finches, be patient—they're on their way.

Similar Species: Male Purple Finch (p. 136) is raspberry-colored and has unstreaked undertail coverts, and the female has brown cheeks contrasting with a white eyebrow and a mustache stripe.

Quick I.D.: sparrow-sized. *Male:* deep red forehead, eyebrow and throat; buffy gray belly; brown cheek; streaked sides and undertail coverts. *Female:* brown overall; streaked underparts; lacks prominent eyebrow.
Size: 5–6 in.

Jan Feb Mar Apr May Jun Jul Aug Sept Oct Nov Dec

American Goldfinch
Carduelis tristis

♂

breeding

In spring, the American Gold-finch swings over fields in its distinctive, undulating flight, and it fills the air with its jubilant *po-ta-to chip* call. This bright, cheery songbird is commonly seen during summer in weedy fields, roadsides and backyards, where it often feeds on thistle seeds. The American Goldfinch delays nesting until June or July to ensure a dependable source of insects, thistles and dandelion seeds to feed its young.

The American Goldfinch is a common backyard bird in parts of the Detroit area, and it is attracted to feeding stations that offer a supply of niger seed. Unfortunately, goldfinches are easily bullied at feeders by larger sparrows and finches. Only goldfinches and Pine Siskins invert for food, however, so a special finch feeder with openings below the perches is ideal for ensuring a steady stream of these 'wild canaries.'

Similar Species: Yellow Warbler (p. 99) does not have black on its forehead or wings. Evening Grosbeak is much larger and has broad white wing patches.

Quick I.D.: smaller than a sparrow. *Breeding male:* black forehead, wings and tail; canary-yellow body; wings show white in flight. *Female* and *Non-breeding male:* no black on forehead; yellow-green overall; black wings and tail.
Size: 4^1/$_2$–5^1/$_2$ in.

Jan Feb Mar Apr May Jun Jul Aug Sept Oct Nov Dec

Northern Cardinal
Cardinalis cardinalis

Never far apart, male and female cardinals softly vocalize to one another not only through the breeding season, but year-round, as if sharing sweet nothings. Their ritualized, beak-to-beak feeding reinforces the romantic appeal and bond of these easily identified birds. Although the regal male does little more than warble to the female while she constructs the nest, his parental duties will soon keep him busy. After the eggs have hatched, the nestlings and the brooding female will remain in the nest while the male provides much of the food for the family.

The Northern Cardinal is becoming more common at backyard feeders, and many homeowners vividly remember the day their yards were first graced by its presence. As if grateful to residents with backyard feeders, Northern Cardinals offer up their bubbly *What cheer! What cheer! Birdie-birdie-birdie What cheer!* to awaken neighborhoods.

Similar Species: Male Scarlet Tanager (p. 113) has a black tail and wings and no crest.

Quick I.D.: smaller than a robin. *Male:* unmistakable; red overall; black mask and throat; pointed crest; red, conical bill. *Female:* similar to male except plumage quite a bit duller. *Immature:* like a female with a dark bill.
Size: 8–9 in.

Jan Feb Mar Apr May Jun Jul Aug Sept Oct Nov Dec

Rose-breasted Grosbeak
Pheucticus ludovicianus

♀

♂

The male Rose-breasted Grosbeak has a voice to match his magnificent plumage. Showing not the least concern for would-be predators, he flaunts his song and plumage in treetop performances. The male's outlandish plumage compensates for that of his unassuming mate, which lacks the formal dress but shares her partner's musical talents. Whether the nest is incubated by the male or the female, the developing young are continually introduced into the world of song by the brooding parent.

This common songster's boldness does not go unnoticed by the appreciative birding community, which eagerly anticipates the male's annual spring concert. This neotropical migrant nests in mature deciduous forests, such as those found in parts of Oakland County.

Similar Species: Male is distinctive. Female is similar to female Purple Finch (p. 136) and sparrows, but is generally larger.

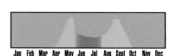

Jan Feb Mar Apr May Jun Jul Aug Sept Oct Nov Dec

Quick I.D.: smaller than a robin.
Male: black hood; rose breast; black back and wings; white rump; white wing bars; light-colored, conical bill. *Female:* heavily streaked with brown; white eyebrow; light-colored, conical bill; light throat.
Size: 7–8 in.

Indigo Bunting
Passerina cyanea

Metallic-blue male Indigo Buntings are frequently encountered in open areas of overgrown fields and along forest edges. Perched atop a shrub or thicket, the males conduct elaborate tactical maneuvers with song. With rival males only a voice away, Indigo Buntings call continuously through the day to maintain superiority over their peers. Neighboring males copy and learn from one another, producing 'song territories.' Each male within a song territory has personal variation to the basic *fire-fire, where-where, here-here, see-it see-it*, producing his own acoustic fingerprint.

Indigo Buntings are widespread throughout our area during summer, popping out of dense bushes anywhere from Stony Creek Metropark to Oakwoods Metropark. They build a small cup nest low to the ground, in an upright crotch in a shrubby tangle. Once nesting duties are complete, these buntings are quick to leave our area, beginning their exodus in late August, after a partial molt.

Similar Species: Eastern Bluebird (p. 91) is larger and has a red breast and a slimmer body. Female is similar to many female sparrows, but lacks the streaking.

breeding

Quick I.D.: sparrow-sized; conical bill. *Male:* turquoise blue plumage; darker wings and tail. *Female:* soft brown overall; hints of blue on rump.
Size: 5¹/₂ in.

Jan Feb Mar Apr May Jun Jul Aug Sept Oct Nov Dec

House Sparrow
Passer domesticus

This common backyard bird often confuses novice birdwatchers because the females and immatures can be very nondescript. The male is relatively conspicuous—he has a black bib, a gray cap and white lines trailing down from his mouth (as though he has spilled milk on himself)—and he sings a continuous series of *cheep-cheep-cheeps*. The best field mark for the female, however, apart from her pale eyebrow, is that there are no distinctive field marks.

The House Sparrow was introduced to North America in the 1850s to control insects. The majority of its diet is seeds, however, and it has become somewhat of a pest. The House Sparrow's aggressive nature usurps several native songbirds from nesting cavities, and its boldness often drives other birds away from backyard feeders. The House Sparrow and the European Starling, two of the most common birds in cities and on farms, are a constant reminder of the negative impact of human introductions on natural systems.

Similar Species: Male is distinctive. Female is similar to female sparrows and finches but tends to lack any distinctive markings.

Jan Feb Mar Apr May Jun Jul Aug Sept Oct Nov Dec

Quick I.D.: mid-sized sparrow; brownish-gray belly. *Male:* black throat; gray forehead; white jowl; chestnut nape. *Female:* plain; pale eyebrow; mottled wings.
Size: 5¹/₂–6¹/₂ in.

Watching Birds

Identifying your first new bird can be so satisfying that you just might become addicted to birdwatching. Luckily, birdwatching does not have to be expensive. It all hinges on how involved in this hobby you want to get. Setting up a simple backyard feeder is an easy way to get to know the birds sharing your neighborhood, and some people simply find birdwatching a pleasant way to complement a nightly walk with the dog or a morning commute into work.

Many people enjoy going to urban parks and feeding the wild birds that have become accustomed to humans. This activity provides people with intimate contact with urban-dwelling birds, but remember that birdseed, or better yet the birds' natural food items, are much healthier for the birds than bread and crackers. As a spokesperson for the animals' health, kindly remind 'bread tossers' of the implications of their actions.

SEASONS OF BIRDWATCHING

Spring

The arrival of spring in Detroit is accompanied by the welcomed sounds and sights of spring migrants. Early arrivals soon become conspicuous as Horned Larks, Red-winged Blackbirds, American Robins and Song Sparrows begin to appear. Resident birds are faced with the task of defending their existing territories, and waterfowl, such as the Common Goldeneye and Red-Breasted Merganser, move through to their northern breeding grounds as soon as the lakes become ice-free. Day by day, the tempo of bird migration escalates. Throughout late April and May, terns, gulls and shorebirds migrate north, while many of the songbirds make their long-awaited first appearances in the Detroit area. May is the peak migration time in southern Michigan, and the rich red maple and ash forests come alive with a bustling of activity. By the end of May, all but a few of the migrants have navigated their way northward, while the permanent summer residents, such as the Eastern Meadowlark and the Chipping Sparrow have settled in. During this time bird baths or running water attracts many birds to our backyards and local parks.

Summer

Although many of our warblers and sparrows are migratory, summers in the Detroit area still offer many sights for the avid birdwatcher. A few lingering migrant shorebirds can still be found through late June, and with an overlap between early and late-nesting bird species, the summer birding season reaches its peak in June. Pointe Mouillee State Game Area is the best place to see herons, egrets, shorebirds and ducks. Although there is generally less movement and activity during summer, the sweet songs of the Scarlet Tanager and the Indigo Bunting are still commonly heard, to the delight of area birdwatchers. The pace of life slows in July; bird song is silenced while young fledglings in juvenile plumage continue to confuse the everyday observer.

Fall

Fall in the Detroit area is a time of great change and fluctuation in local bird populations due to the almost daily arrival and departure of migrants. The fall migrations begin toward the end of summer with the arrival of migratory shorebirds to local marshes, mudflats and occasionally to flooded fields. To the everyday observer, during late August, Common Nighthawks can provide one of the first visible signs of migration as they move through the Detroit area in loose flocks in late afternoon. By the beginning of September, a marked movement of birds can be seen returning from the north. Some species, such as gulls, terns, swallows, cowbirds and bobolinks, might be in sizable flocks. September is also the time to look for the mass migrations of Broad-Winged Hawks and Blue Jays on their travels south. Warblers and thrushes often pass through the area from late August to mid-September. Waterfowl migration is at its height once October arrives. In early November, northwest winds over the Detroit area might bring a local Golden Eagle migration.

Winter

The winter months are a good time to find swans and ducks offshore at Belle Isle. Because Lake St. Clair and the Detroit River do not always freeze over entirely, they often attract a wide variety of waterbirds and waterfowl. A visit to Kensington Metropark in Oakland County might reward the birder with views of many common wintering and permanent resident species, such as the Tufted Titmouse, the Black-capped Chickadee, the Hairy Woodpecker and the Red-bellied Woodpecker. Toward the end of winter, Red-winged Blackbirds and flocks of Tundra Swans begin to appear. Don't forget that winter can be a busy time of year in urban areas. This is definitely the best time to set out your backyard birdfeeder.

BIRDING OPTICS

Most people who are interested in birdwatching will eventually buy a pair of binoculars. They help you identify key bird characteristics, such as plumage and bill color, and they also help you identify other birders! Birdwatchers are a friendly sort, and a chat among birders is all part of the experience.

You'll use your binoculars often, so select a pair that will contribute to the quality of your birdwatching experience—they don't have to be expensive. If you need help deciding which pair would be right for you, talk to other birdwatchers or to someone at your local nature center. Many models are available, and when shopping for binoculars it's important to keep two things in mind: weight and magnification.

One of the first things you'll notice about binoculars (apart from the price extremes) is that they all have two numbers associated with them (8x40, for example). The first number, which is always the smallest, is the magnification (how large the bird will appear), while the second is the size (in millimeters) of the objective lens (the larger end). It might seem important at first to get the highest magnification possible, but a reasonable magnification of 7x–8x is optimal for all-purpose birding, because it draws you fairly close to most birds without causing too much shaking. Some shaking happens to everyone; to overcome it, rest the binoculars against a support, such as a partner's shoulder or a tree.

The size of the objective lens is really a question of birding conditions and weight. Because wider lenses (40–50 mm) will bring in more light, these are preferred for birding in low-light situations (like before sunrise or after sunset). If these aren't the conditions that you will be pursuing, a light pair that has an objective lens diameter of less than 30 mm might be the right choice. Because binoculars tend to become heavy after hanging around your neck all day, the compact models are becoming increasingly popular. If you have a pair that is heavy, you can purchase a strap that redistributes part of the weight to the shoulders and lower back.

Another valuable piece of equipment is a spotting scope. It is very useful when you are trying to sight waterfowl, shorebirds or soaring raptors, but it is really of no use if you are intent on seeing forest birds. A good spotting scope has a magnification of around 40x. It has a sturdy tripod or a window mount for the car. Be wary of second-hand models of telescopes, as they are designed for seeing stars, and their magnification is too great for birdwatching. One of the advantages of having a scope is that you will be able to see far-off birds, which can help during our winters (to see overwintering waterfowl, for example) or during migration (to see shorebirds and raptors). By setting up in one spot (or by not even leaving your car) you can observe faraway flocks that would be little more than specks in your binoculars.

With these simple pieces of equipment (none of which is truly essential) and this handy field guide, anyone can enjoy birds in their area. Many birds are difficult to see because they stay hidden in treetops, but you can learn to identify them by their songs. After experiencing the thrill of a couple of hard-won identifications, you will find yourself taking your binoculars on walks, drives and trips to the beach and cabin. As rewards accumulate with experience, you may find the books and photos piling up and your trips being planned just to see birds!

BIRDING BY EAR

Sometimes, bird listening can be more effective than bird watching. The technique of birding by ear is gaining popularity, because listening for birds can be more efficient, productive and rewarding than waiting for a visual confirmation. Birds have distinctive songs that they use to resolve territorial disputes, and sound is therefore a useful way to identify species. It is particularly useful when trying to watch some of the smaller forest-dwelling birds. Their size and often indistinct plumage can make a visual search of the forest canopy frustrating. To facilitate auditory searches, catchy paraphrases are included in the descriptions of many of the birds. If the paraphrase just doesn't seem to work for you (they are often a personal thing) be creative and try to find one that fits. By spending time playing the song over in your head, fitting words to it, the voices of birds soon become as familiar as the voices of family members. Many excellent CDs and tapes are available at bookstores and wild-bird stores for the songs of the birds in your area.

BIRDFEEDERS

They're messy, they can be costly, and they're sprouting up in neighborhoods everywhere. Feeding birds has become a common pastime in residential communities all over North America. Although the concept is fairly straightforward, as with anything else involving birds, feeders can become quite elaborate.

The great advantage to feeding birds is that neighborhood chickadees, jays, juncos and finches are enticed into regular visits. Don't expect birds to arrive at your feeder as soon as you set it up; it may take weeks for a few regulars to incorporate your yard into their daily routine. As the popularity of your feeder grows, the number of visiting birds will increase and more species will arrive. You will notice that your feeder is busier during the winter months, when natural foods are less abundant. You can increase the odds of a good avian turnout by using a variety of feeders and seeds. When a number of birds habitually visit your yard, maintaining the feeder becomes a responsibility, because the birds may begin to rely on it as a regular food source.

Larger birds tend to enjoy feeding on platforms or on the ground; smaller birds are comfortable on hanging seed dispensers. Certain seeds tend to attract specific birds; nature centers and wild-bird supply stores are the best places to ask how to attract a favorite species. It's mainly seed eaters that are attracted to backyards; some birds have no interest in feeders. Only the most committed birdwatcher will try to attract birds that are insect eaters, berry eaters or, in some extreme cases, scavengers!

The location of the feeder can influence the amount of business it receives from the neighborhood birds. Because birds are wild, they are instinctively wary, and they are unlikely to visit an area where they might come under attack. When putting up your feeder, think like a bird. A good, clear view with convenient escape routes is always appreciated. Cats like birdfeeders that are close to the ground and within pouncing distance from a bush; obviously, birds don't. Above all, a birdfeeder should be in view of a favorite window, where you can sit and enjoy the rewarding interaction of your appreciative feathered guests.

Glossary

accipiter: a forest hawk (genus *Accipiter*); characterized by a long tail and short, rounded wings; feeds mostly on birds.

brood: *n.* a family of young from one hatching; *v.* to sit on eggs so as to hatch them.

coniferous: cone-producing trees, usually softwood evergreens (e.g., spruce, pine, fir).

corvid: a member of the crow family (Corvidae); includes crows, jays, magpies and ravens.

covey: a brood or flock of partridges, quails or grouse.

crop: an enlargement of the esophagus, serving as a storage structure and (in pigeons) has glands which produce secretions.

dabbling: foraging technique used by ducks, where the head and neck are submerged but the body and tail remain on the water's surface.

dabbling duck: a duck that forages by dabbling; it can usually walk easily on land, it can take off without running, and it has a brightly colored speculum; includes Mallards, Gadwalls, teals and others.

deciduous: a tree that loses its leaves annually (e.g., oak, maple, aspen, birch).

dimorphism: the existence of two distinct forms of a species, such as between the sexes.

eclipse: the dull, female-like plumage that male ducks briefly acquire after molting from their breeding plumage.

elbow patches: dark spots at the bend of the outstretched wing, seen from below.

flycatching: feeding behavior where a bird leaves a perch, snatches an insect in mid-air, and returns to their previous perch; also known as 'hawking.'

fledgling: a young chick that has just acquired its permanent flight feathers, but is still dependent on its parents.

flushing: a behavior where frightened birds explode into flight in response to a disturbance.

gape: the size of the mouth opening.

irruption: a sporadic mass migration of birds into a non-breeding area.

larva: a development stage of an animal (usually an invertebrate) that has a different body form from the adult (e.g., caterpillar, maggot).

leading edge: the front edge of the wing as viewed from below.

litter: fallen plant material, such as twigs, leaves and needles, that forms a distinct layer above the soil, especially in forests.

lore: the small patch between the eye and the bill.

molting: the periodic replacement of worn out feathers (often twice a year).

morphology: the science of form and shape.

nape: the back of the neck.

neotropical migrant: a bird that nest in North America, but overwinters in the New World tropics.

niche: an ecological role filled by a species.

open country: a landscape that is primarily not forested.

parasitism: a relationship between two species where one benefits at the expense of the other.

phylogenetics: a method of classifying animals that puts the oldest ancestral groups before those that have arisen more recently.

pishing: making a sound to attract birds by saying pishhh as loudly and as wetly as comfortably possible.

polygynous: having a mating strategy where one male breeds with several females.

polyandrous: having a mating strategy where one female breeds with several males.

plucking post: a perch habitually used by an accipiter for plucking feathers from its prey.

raptor: a carnivorous (meat-eating) bird; includes eagles, hawks, falcons and owls.

rufous: rusty red in color.

speculum: a brightly colored patch in the wings of many dabbling ducks.

squeaking: making a sound to attract birds by loudly kissing the back of the hand, or by using a specially design squeaky bird call.

talons: the claws of birds of prey.

understorey: the shrub or thicket layer beneath a canopy of trees.

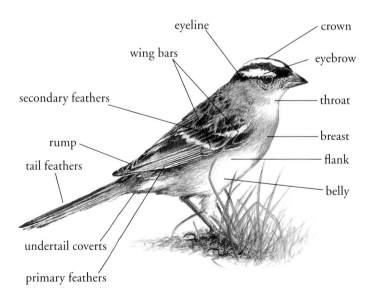

References

American Ornithologists' Union. 1983–97. *Check-list of North American Birds.* 6th ed. (and its supplements). American Ornithologists' Union, Washington, D.C.

Craves, J.A. 1996. *Birds of Southeast Michigan: Dearborn, Wayne County.* Bulletin 62. Cranbrook Institute of Science, Bloomfield Hills, Michigan.

Ehrlich, P.R., D.S. Dobkin and D. Wheye. 1988. *The Birder's Handbook.* Fireside, New York.

Evans, H.E. 1993. *Pioneer Naturalists: The Discovery and Naming of North American Plants and Animals.* Henry Holt and Company, New York.

Farrand, J., ed. 1983. *The Audubon Society Master Guide to Birding.* 3 vols. Alfred A. Knopf, New York.

Gotch, A.F. 1981. *Birds: Their Latin Names Explained.* Blandford Press, Dorset, England.

McPeek, G.A., ed. 1994. *The Birds of Michigan.* Indiana University Press, Bloomington.

Mearns, B., and R. Mearns. 1992. *Audubon to Xantus: The Lives of Those Commemorated in North American Bird Names.* Academic Press, San Diego.

Michigan Audubon Society. 1994. *Bird Finding Guide to Michigan.* Michigan Audubon Society, Lansing.

National Audubon Society. 1971–95. *American Birds.* Vols. 25–48.

Reader's Digest Association. *Book of North American Birds.* The Reader's Digest Association, Pleasantville, New York.

Robbins, C.S., B. Brunn and H.S. Zim. 1966. *Birds of North America.* Golden Press, New York.

Scott, S.S. 1987. *Field Guide to the Birds of North America.* National Geographic Society, Washington, D.C.

Terres, J.K. 1995. *The Audubon Society Encyclopedia of North American Birds.* Wings Books, New York.

Checklist of Detroit-area Birds

This checklist includes a total of 248 bird species recorded in Wayne, Oakland and Macomb counties.

Checklist symbols:

Seasons

W = Winter (mid-December through February)

Sp = Spring (March through early June)

Su = Summer (mid-July through July)

F = Fall (August through December)

Breeding Status

B = Regular breeder (nests every year)

b = Irregular breeder (nests infrequently; few nesting records)

? = Suspected breeder (no confirmation of nesting)

+ = Former breeder (no nesting records in recent years)

Abundance (in appropriate habitats)

C = Common to abundant (always present in large numbers)

F = Fairly common (always present in moderate to small numbers)

U = Uncommon (usually present in small numbers)

R = Rare (observed in very small numbers, and perhaps not every year)

X = Extremely rare (fewer than 10 recorded sightings during that season)

- = Absent (no recorded sightings)

L = Local (occurrence is restricted to a few locations)

e = Erratic (can occur in substantially larger or smaller numbers during certain years)

The checklist species are listed in taxonomic order (in accordance with the 41st supplement [July 1997] of the American Ornithologists' Union's *Check-list of North American Birds*). A blank line separates each family of birds. This checklist does not include 'accidental' species (recorded fewer than 10 times ever in our area).

	W	Sp	Su	F
❑ Red-throated Loon	X	-	-	X
❑ Common Loon	RL	FL	-	UL
❑ Pied-billed Grebe (B)	X	F	F	R
❑ Horned Grebe	RL	UL	-	UL
❑ Red-necked Grebe	X	X	-	X
❑ Double-crested Cormorant (?)	R	C	F	C
❑ American Bittern (BL)	-	U	U	R
❑ Least Bittern (bL)	-	R	R	-
❑ Great Blue Heron (B)	RL	C	C	U
❑ Great Egret (B)	-	U	U	R
❑ Green Heron (B)	-	U	U	-
❑ Black-crowned Night-Heron (bL)	R	F	F	R
❑ Yellow-crowned Night-Heron	-	X	X	-
❑ Turkey Vulture (B)	-	F	U	C
❑ Snow Goose	X	R	-	R
❑ Canada Goose (B)	C	C	C	C
❑ Mute Swan (B)	F	F	F	F
❑ Tundra Swan	-	FL	-	FL
❑ Wood Duck (B)	R	F	F	F
❑ Gadwall	U	F	R	F
❑ American Wigeon	U	F	X	F
❑ American Black Duck (BL)	U	U	R	U
❑ Mallard (B)	C	C	C	C
❑ Blue-winged Teal (B)	X	F	R	F
❑ Northern Shoveler (bL)	R	U	R	U
❑ Northern Pintail	R	U	-	U
❑ Green-winged Teal	R	F	X	F
❑ Canvasback	FL	-	XL	-
❑ Redhead	FL	FL	XL	FL
❑ Ring-necked Duck	R	UL	-	UL
❑ Greater Scaup	UL	UL	-	UL
❑ Lesser Scaup	F	F	XL	F
❑ Oldsquaw	R	R	-	R
❑ Bufflehead	U	U	-	U

	W	Sp	Su	F
❑ Common Goldeneye	F	F	-	F
❑ Hooded Merganser	R	U	-	U
❑ Red-breasted Merganser	R	C	-	C
❑ Common Merganser	C	C	-	C
❑ Ruddy Duck	R	U	X	U
❑ Osprey	-	R	-	U
❑ Bald Eagle (+)	U	U	U	U
❑ Northern Harrier (+)	R	U	-	F
❑ Sharp-shinned Hawk	U	U	-	C
❑ Cooper's Hawk (bL)	U	U	U	F
❑ Northern Goshawk	R	R	-	R
❑ Red-shouldered Hawk (+)	R	U	RL	UL
❑ Broad-winged Hawk (bL)	-	F	RL	C
❑ Red-tailed Hawk (B)	C	C	C	C
❑ Rough-legged Hawk	U	R	-	U
❑ Golden Eagle	X	-	-	UL
❑ American Kestrel (B)	F	F	F	F
❑ Merlin	R	R	-	U
❑ Peregrine Falcon (bL)	-	R	RL	U
❑ Ring-necked Pheasant (B)	U	U	U	U
❑ Ruffed Grouse (BL)	U	U	U	U
❑ Northern Bobwhite (b)	R	R	R	R
❑ Virginia Rail (BL)	X	U	U	U
❑ Sora (BL)	X	F	F	U
❑ Common Moorhen (BL)	-	UL	UL	RL
❑ American Coot (BL)	FL	FL	FL	FL
❑ Sandhill Crane	-	RL	RL	RL
❑ Black-bellied Plover	-	UL	RL	UL
❑ American Golden-Plover	-	UL	-	RL
❑ Semipalmated Plover	-	F	-	F
❑ Killdeer (B)	X	C	C	U

	W	Sp	Su	F
Greater Yellowlegs	-	F	R	F
Lesser Yellowlegs	-	F	R	F
Solitary Sandpiper	-	U	-	U
Spotted Sandpiper (B)	-	F	U	F
Upland Sandpiper	-	RL	RL	RL
Whimbrel	-	R	-	R
Ruddy Turnstone	-	U	-	U
Sanderling	-	U	-	U
Semipalmated Sandpiper	-	FL	RL	FL
Least Sandpiper	-	FL	RL	FL
Pectoral Sandpiper	-	FL	RL	FL
Dunlin	C	FL	-	FL
Stilt Sandpiper	-	U	-	U
Short-billed Dowitcher	-	UL	RL	UL
Long-billed Dowitcher	-	RL	-	RL
Common Snipe (b)	X	F	U	F
American Woodcock (B)	-	F	U	U
Wilson's Phalarope	-	R	-	R
Red-necked Phalarope	-	R	-	R
Bonaparte's Gull	R	F	-	F
Ring-billed Gull (BL)	C	C	C	C
Herring Gull (BL)	C	C	C	C
Lesser Black-backed Gull	R	R	-	R
Glaucous Gull	R	-	-	R
Great Black-backed Gull	F	U	R	U
Caspian Tern	-	U	U	U
Common Tern (BL)	-	F	UL	F
Forster's Tern (BL)	-	C	FL	F
Black Tern (BL)	-	U	U	R
Rock Dove (B)	C	C	C	C
Mourning Dove (B)	C	C	C	C
Black-billed Cuckoo (B)	-	U	U	R
Yellow-billed Cuckoo (B)	-	U	U	R

	W	Sp	Su	F
Eastern Screech-Owl (B)	U	U	U	U
Great Horned Owl (B)	U	U	U	U
Snowy Owl	Ue	-	-	Ue
Barred Owl (b)	UL	UL	UL	UL
Long-eared Owl	R	R	-	R
Short-eared Owl	R	R	-	R
Northern Saw-whet Owl	R	R	-	R
Common Nighthawk (B)	-	U	U	F
Whip-poor-will	-	R	-	-
Chimney Swift (B)	-	C	C	F
Ruby-throated Hummingbird (B)	-	F	U	F
Belted Kingfisher (B)	RL	F	F	U
Red-headed Woodpecker (BL)	R	R	R	R
Red-bellied Woodpecker (B)	F	F	F	F
Yellow-bellied Sapsucker	-	U	-	U
Downy Woodpecker (B)	C	C	C	C
Hairy Woodpecker (B)	C	C	F	C
Northern Flicker (B)	R	C	C	F
Pileated Woodpecker (?L)	RL	RL	RL	RL
Olive-sided Flycatcher	-	U	-	R
Eastern Wood-Pewee (B)	-	F	U	F
Yellow-bellied Flycatcher	-	U	-	U
Acadian Flycatcher (B)	-	U	U	R
Alder Flycatcher (BL)	-	U	RL	R
Willow Flycatcher (B)	-	F	U	R
Least Flycatcher (B)	-	F	R	U
Eastern Phoebe (B)	-	F	U	F

	W	Sp	Su	F
Great Crested Flycatcher (B)	-	F	U	U
Eastern Kingbird (B)	-	F	F	R
Northern Shrike	Re	-	-	Re
White-eyed Vireo	-	R	X	X
Blue-headed Vireo (bL)	-	U	R	U
Yellow-throated Vireo (B)	-	F	U	F
Warbling Vireo (B)	-	C	C	F
Philadelphia Vireo	-	U	-	U
Red-eyed Vireo (B)	-	C	C	F
Blue Jay (B)	F	C	F	C
American Crow (B)	C	F	F	C
Horned Lark (B)	U	F	U	F
Purple Martin (B)	-	U	U	U
Tree Swallow (B)	-	C	C	F
Northern Rough-winged Swallow (B)	-	F	U	F
Bank Swallow (B)	-	F	U	R
Barn Swallow (B)	-	C	C	F
Cliff Swallow (B)	-	U	UL	U
Black-capped Chickadee (B)	C	C	C	C
Boreal Chickadee	X	-	-	-
Tufted Titmouse (B)	C	C	C	C
Red-breasted Nuthatch (BL)	Ue	Ue	RL	Ue
White-breasted Nuthatch (B)	F	F	F	F
Brown Creeper (BL)	R	U	RL	U
Carolina Wren (B)	U	U	U	U
House Wren (B)	-	F	F	R
Winter Wren	X	U	X	U
Sedge Wren (bL)	-	R	R	R
Marsh Wren (BL)	-	U	U	U
Golden-crowned Kinglet	R	F	X	F
Ruby-crowned Kinglet	X	C	-	F
Blue-gray Gnatcatcher (B)	-	F	U	F
Eastern Bluebird (B)	R	U	U	U
Veery (B)	-	F	U	F
Swainson's Thrush	-	F	-	F
Hermit Thrush	R	U	-	U
Wood Thrush (B)	-	U	U	R
American Robin (B)	R	C	C	U
European Starling (B)	C	C	C	C
Gray Catbird (B)	-	F	F	F
Northern Mockingbird (bL)	R	R	R	R
Brown Thrasher (B)	-	U	U	R
American Pipit	-	U	-	U
Cedar Waxwing (B)	U	F	F	F
Blue-winged Warbler (B)	-	U	U	R
Golden-winged Warbler (B)	-	U	U	R
Tennessee Warbler	-	F	-	F
Orange-crowned Warbler	-	U	-	U
Nashville Warbler	-	F	-	U
Northern Parula	-	U	X	R
Yellow Warbler (B)	-	C	F	U
Chestnut-sided Warbler (BL)	-	F	R	U
Magnolia Warbler	-	F	-	C
Cape May Warbler	-	U	-	U
Black-throated Blue Warbler	-	U	-	U
Yellow-rumped Warbler	-	C	-	C
Black-throated Green Warbler (BL)	-	F	X	F
Blackburnian Warbler	-	F	-	U
Pine Warbler (bL)	-	R	R	R

	W	Sp	Su	F
Prairie Warbler	-	R	X	-
Palm Warbler	-	F	-	F
Bay-breasted Warbler	-	F	-	F
Blackpoll Warbler	-	U	-	F
Cerulean Warbler	-	U	U	-
Black-and-white Warbler	-	F	X	F
American Redstart (B)	-	F	R	F
Prothonotary Warbler (b)	-	R	R	-
Worm-eating Warbler	-	R	-	-
Ovenbird (B)	-	F	U	F
Northern Waterthrush (bL)	-	U	R	U
Louisiana Waterthrush (bL)	-	R	R	-
Kentucky Warbler	-	R	X	-
Connecticut Warbler	-	R	-	R
Mourning Warbler (bL)	-	U	R	U
Common Yellowthroat (B)	-	C	C	F
Hooded Warbler	-	R	R	X
Wilson's Warbler	-	F	-	F
Canada Warbler	-	U	-	U
Yellow-breasted Chat (bL)	-	U	R	X
Summer Tanager	-	R	-	-
Scarlet Tanager (B)	-	F	U	U
Eastern Towhee (B)	-	F	U	U
American Tree Sparrow	C	R	-	F
Chipping Sparrow (B)	-	F	F	F
Clay-colored Sparrow (bL)	-	R	X	R
Field Sparrow (B)	-	C	C	F
Vesper Sparrow (B)	-	U	R	R
Savannah Sparrow (B)	-	C	C	U
Grasshopper Sparrow (bL)	-	R	R	R
Henslow's Sparrow (+)	-	R	R	R
Fox Sparrow	-	U	-	U
Song Sparrow (B)	U	C	C	F
Lincoln's Sparrow	-	U	-	U
Swamp Sparrow (B)	R	C	C	F
White-throated Sparrow	R	C	-	C

	W	Sp	Su	F
White-crowned Sparrow	R	F	-	F
Dark-eyed Junco	C	U	-	F
Lapland Longspur	U	R	-	R
Snow Bunting	U	R	-	R
Northern Cardinal (B)	C	C	C	C
Rose-breasted Grosbeak (B)	X	F	U	F
Indigo Bunting (B)	-	C	C	U
Dickcissel	-	Re	Re	-
Bobolink (B)	-	U	U	U
Red-winged Blackbird (B)	R	C	C	F
Eastern Meadowlark (B)	-	F	F	U
Western Meadowlark (b)	-	R	R	R
Rusty Blackbird	X	U	-	F
Brewer's Blackbird	-	R	-	R
Common Grackle (B)	R	C	C	F
Brown-headed Cowbird (B)	R	C	C	F
Orchard Oriole (bL)	-	U	R	-
Baltimore Oriole (B)	-	F	F	U
Pine Grosbeak	Re	-	-	-
Purple Finch	-	Ue	Ue	Fe
House Finch (B)	C	C	C	C
Red Crossbill	Re	-	-	-
White-winged Crossbill	Re	X	X	-
Common Redpoll	Fe	Fe	Ue	Fe
Pine Siskin (b)	Ue	Fe	Ue	Fe
American Goldfinch (B)	C	C	C	C
Evening Grosbeak	Ue	Ue	Ue	Ue
House Sparrow (B)	C	C	C	C

Index of Scientific Names

This index references only primary, illustrated species descriptions.

Index of Common Names

Boldface page numbers refer to primary, illustrated species descriptions.

About the Authors

When he's not out watching birds, frogs or snakes, Chris Fisher researches endangered species management and wildlife interpretation in the Department of Renewable Resources at the University of Alberta. The appeal of western wildlife and wilderness has led to many travels. He is the author of *Birds of Seattle* and co-author of *Birds of Los Angeles, Birds of San Francisco* and *Birds of Denver,* and he still has more books up his sleeve. By sharing his enthusiasm and passion for wild things through lectures, photographs and articles, Chris strives to foster a greater appreciation for the value of our wilderness.

Allen Chartier began birding at age 11, and by the time he was 18, he had a 'life list' of 400 species. In addition to being one of the Detroit area's more active birders, Allen has expanded his birding horizons around the world. He has led birding tours in Michigan, as well as in Texas, Mexico, Costa Rica and Ecuador. Allen is a co-founder of the Holiday Beach Migration Observatory (in nearby Ontario), and he has been a compiler and counter of bird migration there for 22 years. He is also compiler for Wayne County for the annual North American Migration Count, held in May. Allen wrote *Hawks of Holiday Beach,* as well as several articles and papers published in birding journals. Since 1995, Allen has been the managing editor of *Michigan Birds and Natural History,* Michigan's primary ornithological/birding journal, and he is currently preparing a bird-finding guide to southeastern Michigan.